UNIVERSITY LIBRARY
W. S. U. - STEVENS POINT

TEACHING INEFFICIENT LEARNERS

TEACHING INEFFICIENT LEARNERS

By

WINEVA MONTOOTH GRZYNKOWICZ, Ed. D.

*Associate Professor of Special Education
Wisconsin State University
Eau Claire, Wisconsin*

With a Contribution by

Frances Marling, M. Ed.

*Learning Disabilities Teacher
Morton Grove, Illinois*

CHARLES C THOMAS • PUBLISHER
Springfield • Illinois • U.S.A.

Published and Distributed Throughout the World by
CHARLES C THOMAS • PUBLISHER
BANNERSTONE HOUSE
301-327 East Lawrence Avenue, Springfield, Illinois, U.S.A.
NATCHEZ PLANTATION HOUSE
735 North Atlantic Boulevard, Fort Lauderdale, Florida, U.S.A.

This book is protected by copyright. No part of it may be reproduced in any manner without written permission from the publisher.

© 1971, by CHARLES C THOMAS • PUBLISHER
Library of Congress Catalog Card Number: 70-143740

With THOMAS BOOKS *careful attention is given to all details of manufacturing and design. It is the Publisher's desire to present books that are satisfactory as to their physical qualities and artistic possibilities and appropriate for their particular use.* THOMAS BOOKS *will be true to those laws of quality that assure a good name and good will.*

Printed in the United States of America
PP-22

PREFACE

Teaching Inefficient Learners is an attempt to draw together into one textbook the problems of several different areas of special education for the purpose of pinpointing common learning problems. A child does not come to school labelled and classified, and it often takes educators two or three years to condition him so that he will fit into one of our preestablished categories. This book is an attempt to help teachers meet the needs of every child in the room regardless of his label.

It is to be hoped that teachers will learn to recognize and meet the individual needs of each child in the room. No longer should children be expected to fit the school's prescribed curriculum. In this way we should be able to ameliorate and/or prevent many obstacles to learning.

Wineva Montooth Grzynkowicz

ACKNOWLEDGMENTS

I am indebted to all of my former students, especially the graduate students at National College of Education. They have all been instrumental in my learning.

A debt of gratitude must be expressed for my parents, Dr. and Mrs. J. L. Montooth, who inspired me and taught me. The example which they set can never be duplicated.

I owe a very special expression of my appreciation to my husband and our son Steven. Without their encouragement and patience this book could never have been written.

For their assistance in the preparation of this manuscript, I wish to thank Winifred Weldon, Marion Thorson, and Connie Armstrong. I would also like to thank Cherie Miller and William Boyken of Community State Bank in Eau Claire for their assistance and cooperation in the preparation of the final draft.

W.M.G.

CONTENTS

	Page
Preface	v
Acknowledgments	vii

Chapter

I.	INEFFICIENT LEARNERS	1
II.	PHILOSOPHICAL FOUNDATIONS FOR A MULTISENSORY APPROACH TO REMEDIATION	15
III.	A PSYCHOLOGICAL BASIS FOR SENSE TRAINING *Frances Marling*	32
IV.	TWENTIETH CENTURY THEORIES OF EDUCATIONAL METHODS FOR INEFFICIENT LEARNERS	41
V.	THE TEACHER OF INEFFICIENT LEARNERS	56
VI.	CLASSROOM MANAGEMENT	67
VII.	DIAGNOSTIC TOOLS AND PRESCRIPTIVE PLANNING	76
VIII.	PREVENTION OF LEARNING PROBLEMS	108
Appendix A.	Instructional Material Sources	116
Appendix B.	Suggested Readings	133
Index		136

TEACHING INEFFICIENT LEARNERS

Chapter I

INEFFICIENT LEARNERS

THE NUMBER of different areas of special education has been constantly increasing. Those children whose handicap was the most obvious were the first to receive our attention. We have noticed the child whose mentality was quite different from others of the same age group. These we have classified for the purpose of special education into two subgroups: those who are trainable and those who are educable. We have recognized the other extreme and called them gifted. The physically handicapped children, those with chronic medical problems, and the crippled are not difficult to identify. Other groups we have identified are the blind, partially sighted, deaf, and hard of hearing. Special educational services have also been provided for those who have speech problems.

These classifications left us with many children who obviously needed help, but we did not know quite how to label them, which seems to be a prerequisite to teaching them. Often they have been classified as maladjusted, underachievers, emotionally disturbed, or culturally disadvantaged, simply for want of a better term.

In the past, it was the responsibility of the classroom teacher to teach whatever children were assigned to her with little labelling and classifying. Today, with our emphasis on specialization and classification of teachers and students, we tend to overdiagnose and overlabel, often erroneously. This is always justified by the need to meet certain requirements and hence qualify for financial assistance which we naively assume will solve many of our problems.

Newer labels which have been attached to children who do not seem to be learning as we believe they should are the following: the underachiever, culturally disadvantaged, socially malajusted, and learning disability. Although it is recognized that there is no clear-cut dividing line between these groups, each will be considered separately to demonstrate that they have common problems which interfere with learning.

THE UNDERACHIEVER

The *underachiever* is one of the newer terms being used in special education. By itself the term is so descriptive that anyone hearing it has an immediate picture of a child who is not doing what it seems to the observer he should be able to do. We picture a child who has an average or above average score on the intelligence tests that were given. He seems to have no special problem except that he is not doing average work in school. He usually has marks on his grade sheet that indicate he is not working up to ability or that he could do better. If this child is in the lower grades, we see him as a child who is able to do things that he seems to like to do but just will not, according to his teacher, do the assigned academics. He can find other things to do or can waste time so that he just does not get around to the paper work. He may sit and daydream or draw endless pictures. This child is too often called lazy or a dreamer because the teacher believes that all the equipment necessary for learning is present.

We have become so involved with test scores that the child has become a commodity to be manipulated rather than a raw material to be refined. The child who does not conform to our pattern is marked as an underachiever and we dislike the thought that our expectations or our methods might need to be altered to fit the needs of the child.

If the underachieving child is in a high school where all the children are gifted and all are expected to attend college, then he has little chance of ever achieving his potential, whatever it may be. He is compared to parents, siblings, and peers and made to believe that he is a great disappointment to the family and community. With continued unorganized persecution, he may become so confused that he will require his own psychiatrist, which is some sort of status symbol.

In a high school with less pressure on all fronts, this child who has not been helped is often the dropout who quits to go to work or becomes a delinquent. Some of the underachievers do finish school and graduate. Some may even attend college but perform much less efficiently than they might have been expected to perform. These have made their own adjustments without our help and they are no credit to our educational system—rather they are a discredit. With a little assistance from educators, they might have accomplished much more.

The percentage of children in our educational systems who do not perform up to our level of expectation should be of vital concern to every educator. Rather than spend the preponderance of our time and money on those who are in the upper 2 percent of the high school classes and concentrating on a huge honors award night we should give some attention to the dropout rate. We need to find out why the student is not achieving and help him overcome the problem, whatever it is, without concentrating on a label or category.

Causation

It would seem highly improbable that there is actually such a thing as an underachiever, although this may be a question of semantics. Most children enter school expecting to learn until we use the first six weeks to destroy this idea. We ask the child to complete tasks for which he is not ready and expect him to do abstractions beyond his ability. Rather than adjust our curriculum and our educational objectives to him and his needs we start him on his path to underachievement which will be perpetuated throughout his school life.

It appears that the term "underachiever" is a convenient misnomer for a large group of children. Most children are producing as well as they are able to with their own unique set of problems. They actually are achieving as well as they are able to do at this time, with these obstacles. If we could take a good look at the problems of these children we might find that they are producing quite well.

Here it is suggested that some problems are common to many different special categories of children. There could very conceivably be a developmental lag that has gone unobserved. There might have been an experiential deficit, sensory deprivation, and certainly inappropriate educational provision. Any one of these obstacles is sufficient to cause a child to perform at a lower level than we believe he should.

THE SOCIALLY MALADJUSTED

In considering the *socially maladjusted* child it must be initially recognized that all children do not react identically to any given situation or set of circumstances, nor should they be expected to do so. By the time a child has reached school age he has had to learn how to satisfy his needs in his own unique environment. Different environments have different standards and different methods of enforcing these standards. It is small wonder then that we find such a wide range of personality development has begun when the child arrives at school. Stealing may be a sign of social maladjustment or it may be the accepted method of filling a need. What appears to the teacher to be maladjustment may, in fact, be learned and taught adjustment. On the other hand, stealing may be a sign of a serious emotional disturbance. Each child and his circumstances are different and should be so considered. This makes any clear-cut description of characteristic behavior or symptoms of maladjustment practically an impossibility.

The difference between maladjustment and emotional disturbance which is sufficient to warrant special class placement seems to be a matter of degree. Here we are concerned with socially maladjusted children and not the seriously disturbed; however, the same signs and characteristic behavior may be observed. Although the list of adjustment mechanisms might seem endless, some of the more common observable characteristics will be described. It should be remembered that the behavior itself is neither good nor bad, the degree to which it is used is the important factor.

Some Characteristics of Maladjusted Children

Tics or nervous spasms such as facial twitching or a jerking of various parts of the body. This may be confined to one particular area or it may vary in location. Another variation might be foot tapping, finger drumming, hair twisting, nail biting, or scratching.

Digestive disturbances such as frequent vomiting, upset stomach, colitis, ulcers, or other similar symptoms.

Poor speech patterns such as rapid or nervous speech, stuttering, or baby talk.

Restlessness or fidgeting and an apparent inability to sit still, stand still, or be still. Accompanying this is an inability to remain attentive for very long at a time.

Aggressiveness and a tendency to find trouble where no trouble existed. The apparent desire to start trouble. Even though the child might have the same goal as other children he may take the opposite view just to be contrary.

Bullying may be an extension of the previously listed behavior but it is often more noticeable by teachers.

Dishonesty includes lying, cheating, and stealing.

Disturbances in sleep patterns include nightmares and sleepwalking. While not observable by the teacher, they are often reported to her by the parent or child.

Sensitivity to such a degree that feelings are hurt too easily. The child is apt to cry too easily, laugh too easily, and be hurt too much.

Withdrawal tendencies may be observed in the shy, quiet child who tries not to get involved in any activity.

Excessive emotional displays such as temper tantrums, pouting, hating too much, loving too hard, worrying too much, or fearing too much.

Poor schoolwork is often the symptom most obvious to the teacher. Although the child appears to be capable, he often does not produce acceptably in the classroom.

Causation

The list of causes for social maladjustment would be as long as the list of children so afflicted. Since there are many works done on this topic, the reader is referred to other sources to pursue this topic in depth. As in other classifications of children with learning problems, etiology is useful to the teacher only in that it might assist in remediation or prevention. The causes to be considered here briefly are those which are the fault of our educational system and which we can adjust for possible remediation.

The socially maladjusted children that we meet in our classrooms have learned to resolve their conflicts in what is to us an unacceptable manner. These conflicts may have been between their needs and the values of their own environment, or between their needs and our unrealistic, inflicted environment. Whatever the cause of the conflict, we need to help the child find acceptable means of adjusting.

It would seem that many children are being subjected to an inappropriate education because the goals are unrealistic. The child who must read about the happy middle-class home while he is thinking of his own home, which is quite different, is receiving inappropriate education which can compound his problem. When we expect all children to learn to read and write at the same time because they have lived the same number of years we have unrealistic goals which may lead to conflict and poor adjustment. The child who is unable to meet our demands must find some way to react that is unacceptable as there is no acceptable way to fail. The child who lags behind his peers developmentally is bound to fail.

The child with an experiential deficit and the one whose senses have not been adequately developed must likewise find some means of avoiding the impossible demands we persist in making. The poor child whose ears are not accustomed to fine discriminations is expected to immediately learn the difficult vowels. If he cannot, he must find some way to avoid the impossible.

Although many of the causes of maladjustment in children are beyond the scope of the educator, many remain to which we should give attention. We need to set more realistic goals, be concerned with developmental lags, experiential deficits, and sensory deprivation.

THE CULTURALLY DISADVANTAGED

The term *culturally disadvantaged* would seem to be a very poor choice of words to use in describing a large group of children who do not fit neatly into any other special category. It is most difficult to arrive at any commonality of this group of children as there are many ways to look at culture.

Culture could be used to mean that which is believed to be of higher quality or greater refinement. This is the meaning we refer to when we speak of music, art, and literature as representing culture. If this is the connotation given to culturally disadvantaged as a facet of special education, we should surely include a very large segment of our school population. Obviously this is not what we mean when we speak of culturally disadvantaged school children.

A Definition Is Difficult

The sociological meaning of culture is more fitting to a definition of the group of children we refer to as culturally disadvantaged. Here we mean by culture anything that is transmitted from one generation to another. This includes their knowledge, belief, art, morals, law, and mode of survival. We must include habits and traditions. Therefore we can never say "culturally deprived," as there is a definite culture which is transmitted from one generation to the next.

We have come to recognize that many children who live in homes that have a minimum of requirements for economic existence and seem to be impoverished do not do very well in school. We then assume that the reason for the poor schoolwork is the cultural disadvantage of the environment.

It has not seemed to occur to us that the problem in learning is not always and not necessarily the result of the type of home in which the child lives. Many children from an impoverished environment have done quite well in school and in life. Fortunately, there was no one interested enough to impress upon Abraham Lincoln that he had an impoverished background and that he was culturally disadvantaged.

No Child Is Deprived of a Culture

Since culture is a part of our life, and all societies transmit some learnings from generation to generation, no one is deprived. Ordinarily we mean that the child is disadvantaged as compared to the mean of our middle-class structure. We refer to home life, education, books, formal language, and family income. We infer that children from poor homes are impoverished and at a disadvantage in academic work because of the home and environment.

When we attempt to profile the child we class as culturally disadvantaged we immediately get a picture of a child from a home that has very little in the way of material goods. We envision a child from a broken home or one with several and varied father figures. Often we think of these children as constantly being hungry and less strong physically than their middle-class peers. A part of the recurring picture is the struggle for existence, the gangs, and the fights which seem to be accepted as a necessary segment of the culture.

The picture of our disadvantaged child is completed when we add overcrowded classrooms in old unrepaired buildings with teachers who are not there by choice. We group these children all as culturally disadvantaged and assume that the home must be changed before we can aid the child. The task then seems to be insurmountable. We should instead attend to the obstacle to his inefficient learning.

The Experiential Deficit Is Obvious

The child may not have had the same opportunity to learn language from his family that the middle-class child has had. He has learned to communicate but not with enough elaboration to extend his vocabulary. He has probably had little opportunity to acquire a recognition of the necessity for reading. Books have not been important in his life. They are not even worth stealing as there is no available market for converting them into money. The value of money is only for securing the needs of today—tomorrow is not to be considered as it may not come. Only immediate needs command attention.

If the cause of the childs' learning problem is an experential deficit, then the deficit must be ameliorated before adequate efficient academic learning can be accomplished.

Developmental Lags Are Not Unique To Any Culture

A child who has a slow rate of development might be more obvious in a family that is cognizant of the importance of this factor in learning. This family might be more able to cope with the problem than a family in which existence is of prime importance. A lag in development may be the cause for a learning problem for the child from any kind of environment. This then should be considered as a possible cause for inefficiency in learning by the culturally disadvantaged child. Rather than blame the environment and "wash our hands" of the problem, we should make an attempt to alleviate the cause.

Sensory Deprivation Is a Cause of Many Learning Problems

Although children may be born with the sense organs intact, they may not all develop to the degree that is necessary for academic achievement. Sensory deprivation is not confined to any particular socioeconomic class of people. It can be a learning problem for rich or poor, black or white.

Many children live in homes where things are so expensive that they must not be touched, felt, or tasted. Clocks are so valuable that they can no longer be taken apart, cleaned with kerosene on a chicken feather and returned in working condition to the wall. Instead they must be sent to a specialist. There are no trestles to cross, or rails to walk, and no place to make mud pies. Of course it is unthinkable to play train with the kitchen chairs because we would need a specialist to repair the floor. It is not necessary to salvage old parts to build a radio because the head of the house will go to his office and make enough money to buy a new transistor model. If exercise is prescribed, the maid is available for a walk.

There are toys that call attention to details and make the brain perceive what the eye sees. Many parents point out to the child the likenesses and differences of objects. The brain learns to perceive through the eyes, ears, and body, and to rely on all the receptors for adequate information.

Children who have few toys or no toys to learn with are deprived of stimulation. If the parents are too busy or too unconcerned to provide this early stimulation, then the child is deprived of learnings which are fundamental to academic achievement.

For children who are accustomed to a blend of many loud noises which they have learned to ignore, the fine auditory discrimination necessary for phonics is most difficult. It is easy to tune out the teacher entirely.

Inappropriate Education Is Inexcusable

We acknowledge the causes for inefficient learning of the child from a culture that is different, but we do very little about changing our teaching style to accomodate the deficiencies. We would rather blame the home and environment and attempt to change that than simply change our methods and techniques.

We assume that bussing a child from his home environment to some middle-class "desirable environment" will be the magic wand that makes the difference between success and failure. This has only proven to the child that his environment is inferior. He still has to go home to live. We then believe that moving the home will accomplish our goals. It would be very nice and a simple answer if this would be the solution—but the children are still here, in the classroom today, and we must help them.

We are providing inadequate educational facilities when we expect all children to be ready to read and do modern mathematics at a given grade level. We are also providing inadequate educational facilities when we force teachers to accept assignments in classrooms against their wishes. There must be teachers who understand children and how they learn who want to help these children acquire the needed prerequisites to academic learning.

LEARNING DISABILITIES

The labelling of this previously unclassified group of children has given rise to so much confusion regarding terminology that the National Society for Crippled Children and Adults and the Institute of Neurological Diseases and Blindness have made an attempt to clarify the terms. Phase One of this project reported that a review of the literature revealed a total of thirty-eight terms used to describe the children. These are listed as follows.

Group I

Organic Aspects
Associated Deficit Pathology
Organic Brain Damage
Organic Brain Disease
Organic Brain Dysfunction
Minimal Brain Damage
Diffuse Brain Damage
Neurophonia
Organic Driveness
Cerebral Dysfunction

Organic Behavior Disorder
Choreiform Syndrome
Minor Brain Damage
Minimal Brain Injury
Minimal Cerebral Injury
Minimal Chronic Brain Syndrome
Minimal Cerebral Damage
Minimal Cerebral Palsy
Cerebral Dysynchronization Syndrome

Group II

Segment or Consequence
Hyperkinetic Behavior Syndrome
Character Impulse Disorder
Hyperkinetic Impulse Disorder
Aggressive Behavior Disorder
Psychoneurological Learning Disorders
Hyperkinetic Syndrome
Dyslexia
Hyperexcitability Syndrome
Perceptual Cripple

Primary Reading Retardation
Specific Reading Disability
Clumsy Child Syndrome
Hypokinetic Syndrome
Perceptually Handicapped
Aphasoid Syndrome
Learning Disabilities
Conceptually Handicapped
Attention Disorders
Interjacent Child

This group adopted the term *minimal brain dysfunction syndrome* and defined it as referring to ". . . children of near average, average, or above average general intelligence with certain learning or behavorial disabilities ranging from mild to severe, which are associated with deviations of functions of the nervous system."

In spite of this attempt to choose a label that would be consistently used for a group of special children, the term chosen has not been widely accepted. There may be many reasons for this hesitancy to adopt the term but the one voiced most often is that it implies something wrong with the brain and is therefore an unpleasant stigma which should be avoided. The term which implies the least stigma and is more widely used by educators is *learning disabilities*. It will be used in this work to refer to the child who has near normal, normal, or above normal intellectual ability but is at least two years retarded academically.

Although there is little agreement on the choice of the term to be used to label this group of children there is more consistency in the descriptions of the characteristic behavior exhibited by the child. Some of the characteristics of children with learning disabilities will be described but it must be borne in mind that not all children exhibit all of these characteristics. Although some of these characteristics would seem to be normal for young children, they are not normal when they persist beyond the age when other children have outgrown them.

Characteristics of Children with Learning Disabilities

Perseveration—the inability to relinquish an activity after it has reached its culmination. There is difficulty in shifting from one activity to another. Children usually are able to dispense with an activity when they have reached the satisfaction they sought, but the child who perseverates continues the activity after the stimulus has been reduced or removed. This child may make a page full of the same letter or word. He may persist in doing the same problem over and over. He just cannot stop.

Distractibility—the inability to concentrate on the appropriate stimulus. When new stimuli are introduced and selection is necessary, there is too much distraction and the child tries to respond to all the stimuli. This child is distracted by noises, sounds, lights, or objects. He has difficulty making choices and seems unable to endure confusion. This often leads to the next characteristic.

Disinhibition—the inability to control response to extraneous stimuli. This child tries to engage in too many activities and becomes frustrated because he completes none. This can lead to hyperactivity or hypoactivity.

Hyperactivity—an ability to control the degree of reaction to stimuli. This child cannot sit still, stand still, or do anything for very long. He seems to have an overabundant supply of energy.

Hypoactivity—the absence of physical activity. This child sits, stands, or sleeps endlessly.

Emotional instability—lack of emotional control as the term implies. This child reacts emotionally with little reason or control. He laughs too loudly, cries too hard, and does whatever he feels like doing with few thoughts of consequences. He becomes too excited or too disappointed. He is apt to have temper tantrums and then be too sorry.

Perceptual disorders—There are many types of perceptual disorders. There may be a figure-ground distortion. Here the child does not know which to copy from the board—the white marks or the black spaces. There may be difficulty in form discriminations—the recognition of differences in shapes such as between a square and a circle or between the letters *c* and *a*. There may be difficulty in form constancy. The letter on the board may look different to the child when he sees it on paper. There may also be a problem in recognizing forms that have been rotated in space. The child may not know a square as a square if it has been rotated at a forty-five degree angle. There may be a problem in the perception of space and spatial relationships. This is the inability to judge size, distance, boundaries, and the child's own relationship to space. This child is "lost" in space. He may walk into the door because he did not know how far it was from him.

Motor disturbances—may range from poor coordination to cerebral palsy. The disturbance may not be noticed but may still lead to a learning problem. The child may appear awkward and clumsy. He may trip and fall more often than other children in the class. His motor problem may not be evident, but might be discovered through the use of the testing procedures described in Chapter IV.

Speech and language disorders—a difficulty with one or more of the means of communication. This may range from delayed speech or retarded language development to one or more of the "aphasias." The teacher may note difficulty in communication and suspect poor hearing, defective speech, poor auditory discrimination, lack of understanding of word meanings, or poor association of words with symbols.

Conceptual difficulties—difficulty with reasoning and abstractions. This child seems to think concretely and does not make relevant associations. He does not see the humor in jokes, does not "get the idea" of a story, and cannot read "between the lines."

We could list inappropriate aggressiveness, excessive talking, destructiveness, social immaturity, insecurity, catastrophic reactions, excessive daydreaming, fatigability, poor retention, unusual irritability, detail consciousness, poor body image, and many more, but a complete list of characteristics would be almost impossible to compile, since each child with a learning disability seems to contribute more characteristics to the list. Actually the list will not be complete until we have described the last child with a learning disability.

Causation

If we can accept the label *learning disabilities* to include all children with problems in learning for whom there is no special classification at present, then we must recognize that the list of causes could be as complex as the list of labels in present use. By using the term *learning disabilities* we are not limited to considering such specific causation as we would be if our label were *brain-injured* or *neurologically impaired*.

Organic damage can include injury or damage to the brain before, during, or after birth. This would include any irregularity in the oxygen supply, prolonged labor, use of obstetrical instruments, Rh compatibility, rubella, and unusual delivery. Damage can result from unusually high temperatures, diseases, reactions to drugs, and accidents.

Other than these definite causes for damage to the brain, there are many reasons for a child of average intellectual ability to be two or more years retarded academically.

If we acknowledge the fact that there are developmental lags, it seems most incongruous that many primary teachers expect the same level of performance from each child in the room regardless of his level of development. We hear first grade teachers complain about children in the class (especially boys) who cannot do the assigned work. One common complaint is "he is too immature."

It seems to be a common practice that we should not place these developmentally immature children in a special program unless they are at least two years retarded academically or unless the parent consents. The unfortunate child who was too immature for kindergarten and too immature for first grade may then proceed in orderly sequence through the other grades, remaining too immature if someone does not provide the help he needs. He may get far enough to become a high school dropout. Much of this could be avoided.

Learning disabilities are not confined to any particular grade level. Many of the learning disabilities that we see in the upper grades and high school might have been overcome if proper educational approaches had been utilized earlier, but that does not negate the responsibility of the school in providing treatment at any level. The high school student who cannot read well and is given a failing grade because he cannot write a research paper has little choice—he is forced to drop out.

Children who have no serious problems may progress through any kind of educational environment with no obvious ill effects, but what might they have accomplished in a different environment? For a child with any kind of disability, an inappropriate environment may well be the one that allows too much freedom, is too permissive, and provides too much stimulation. The child with a learning disability needs and deserves structure. Often a reduction of stimuli is good remedial procedure. The other extreme—the authoritative leader who expects every child to conform and do the same thing at the same time also provides an inappropriate environment. Inappropriate educational facilities can often cause learning disabilities. Unrealistic goals that cannot be met can only cause further problems. Failure to allow for possible experiential deficits and lack of sensory stimulation will compound the learning problems.

We will, in this work, be concerned with those causes of learning problems which are pertinent to the public school system. Our interest is in those children who can be helped in the schools by teachers who are truly interested in making the effort

Chapter II

PHILOSOPHICAL FOUNDATIONS FOR A MULTISENSORY APPROACH TO REMEDIATION

THE LAST DECADE has seen much literature and professional activity directed toward increasing the body of knowledge concerning disadvantaged learners and methods for teaching them. As increased numbers of these children are identified by means of a refinement in diagnostic techniques, the importance of this group of children will be an overwhelming force in our educational system.

The preponderance of concern regarding the importance of effective sense training for this group of children is evident in a review of current methods of teaching. In studying various philosophers, past and present, there is agreement among many that sense training plays a vital role in the education of the child. Comenius, Locke, and Rousseau were not concerned with special learning problems, Pestalozzi was concerned with waifs, and Itard and Sequin with mentally deficient children, yet many of their educational methods are recommended for teachers of disadvantaged learners.

An eclectic approach is taken, in that the concern is for educational principles of teaching methods, rather than a concern for views regarding metaphysics, values, or ethics.

The philosophers and educational theorists who will be reviewed are Comenius, Locke, Rousseau, Pestalozzi, Itard, and Sequin, who were chosen because of their concern for sense training.

John Amos Comenius (1592-1670)

In *The Great Didactic* Comenius outlined his theories of education. He urged that the teacher appeal to the child's sensory perceptions and that the teacher use materials based on the child's own experience. This same approach was taken in his *Orbis Pictus,* or *World of Pictures.* In the preface, he gave the philosophical principle which guided his works. He believed that everything in the intellect has first existed in the senses. Schools insist on giving pupils things to learn without preparatory sense training and this, he believed, caused many of the problems children have in learning.

Since this is one of the newer approaches to teaching children with learning problems, it would appear to justify a study of the method of teaching advocated by Comenius.

In *The Great Didactic* Comenius gave nine universal principles of instruction. The first of these, "Nature observes a suitable time," concludes that we must begin to educate the child in his early childhood, that subjects are to be arranged to fit the age of the learner, and that nothing be presented to the child which is beyond his comprehension to learn.

His second principle, "Nature prepares the material, before she begins to give it form," implies that the teacher as well as the learner must be ready. Understanding is taught before expression, examples come before rules and we then must proceed from the concrete to the abstract.

From his third principle we can recognize the need for readiness again. "Nature chooses a fit subject to act upon, or first submits one to a suitable treatment in order to make it fit." Before we introduce a new topic or subject we should make the student ready to learn the new material.

The fourth educational principle of Comenius, "Nature is not confused in its operation, but in its forward progress advances distinctly from one point to another," implores us to concentrate on one new learning at a time.

In a plea for teachers to know all methods by which a child is able to learn he stated in the fifth principle, "In all the operations of nature development is from within." We should teach the child to understand and remember before we attempt writing and grammar. "Nature in its formative processes, begins with the universal and ends with the particular," explains to teachers that children should learn the general ideas of a subject before attempting to master all the fine details.

Although his seventh principle may seem outdated in our modern educational systems it is of utmost importance to teachers of children with learning disabilities. "Nature makes no leaps, but proceeds step by step." All studies must be carefully graded, and no child is to proceed to a more difficult task until he has mastered the prerequisite.

The time is to be carefully divided, so that the school year is planned to detail. This is to assure that nothing is omitted or presented out of sequence.

Comenius admonished those students who would quit before completing the task or play truant and encouraged them to be diligent in pursuit of an education in the eighth principle. "If nature commences anything, it does not leave off until the operation is completed." At the same time he insisted that the school must cooperate by locating in a quiet spot, away from distractions.

In the ninth principle he gave attention to textbooks. "Nature carefully avoids obstacles and things likely to cause hurt." He said that scholars should be given no books except those suitable for their classes. He would avoid controversial subjects until the scholar had sufficient learning to be competent to judge wisely. He also said that the scholar should be kept from bad companions in the school and its vicinity.

In facilitating his principles Comenius had advice for the teacher, parents, and the educational system in general.

Comenius advised against a student having more than one teacher in each subject and recommended that education begin early. Motivation is important and education need not be unpleasant. The school is to be a pleasant place, and the teacher is to be a gentle person who can win affection of the pupils as they will then be better able to learn. Parents and teachers alike are exhorted to praise rather than punish. Rewards may be given to the very young, while praise is sufficient for the older student. Visual aids are to be encouraged and a playground is considered a necessity.

If rules must be given they must be given in the shortest and clearest form possible and must be accompanied by examples. Pupils should be forced to memorize as little as possible and then only if understanding comes first. Instruction should be given through the five senses as far as possible as it will be better retained.

John Locke (1632-1704)

In his *Essay Concerning Human Understanding*, John Locke proposed that the human mind is a blank sheet of paper (*tabula rasa*) on which experiences are to engrave knowledge. He maintained that all reason and knowledge are sensation and reflection. Our senses convey to the mind several perceptions of things. Then the mind must do something with these sensations and perceptions take place. These perceptions are the result of an accumulation of previous sensations and involve thinking, doubting, believing, reasoning, and knowing.

In Locke's philosophical teaching then is found the principle that the sense organs of children should be exercised in school. Like Comenius, Locke realized the importance of motivation and rewards for satisfactory performance. He realized the possibilities offered by educating through play. This is not to imply that learning must all be fun, rather that it need not be unpleasant at all times. He believed that education might be play and recreation for children rather than a task if it were presented to them in the correct fashion. There may be dice, playthings, and many other techniques found so that learning could be a sport.

Locke described a method of teaching the alphabet to children by using a game, or as we might call it, a teaching aid. He would have the teacher introduce just two letters first, then gradually add to the number until the complete alphabet had been mastered. The energy and time children spend on playing games may as well be games that can teach at the same time. The teacher is warned to make the first letters presented to the child of a large size and to keep games interesting by removing them for a time. The teacher is reminded not to drive the child to learn to read but to "cheat him into it" if necessary. Readiness was stressed by Locke as he believed it would be better for a child to be a year later learning to read than to start before he is ready and thus develop a dislike for learning.

The method of teaching writing described by Locke is accepted as a modern method of teaching brain-injured children. He would have the teacher teach the child to hold the pencil correctly first because no one should be expected to learn two things at the same time. The child would be taught to follow grooved lines shaped like letters. He would do much tracing and copying before being expected to practice without a copy.

Locke was concerned with the relationship between teacher and learner and thought it was most important for the teacher to establish an environment in which the child could learn without fear of rebuke or punishment. The teacher must be able to get and keep the attention of the scholar, and do so agreeably. When children were showing signs of having difficulty, it was the responsibility of the teacher to stop and help them so that they could master one thing before going on to a more difficult one. There would be a structuring of the class and gentle discipline.

In recognizing individual differences, Locke noted that each man's mind has some peculiarity, and there are scarcely two children who can be educated by the same method. Locke's plan for education of children from lower classes would be questioned in our democratic society even though some aspects of it might be preferable to our limited educational plan for these children. Locke favored a plan whereby these children would be taken from their parents, to be educated in working schools from the ages of three to fourteen. The advantage of this plan would be its economy and efficiency.

The attention given to supplying knowledge through the senses and the environment as advocated by Locke had a profound effect on later educators who began to pay attention to sense training rather than faculty training.

Jean-Jacques Rousseau (1712-1778)

One of the most vocal champions of the rights of children was Jean-Jacques Rousseau. He enlarged upon Locke's concepts by adjusting education to the child. In the preface to *Emile,* he appeals to the reader to learn more about children and not to consider them as miniature adults. For example, Rousseau believed that only by the child's own movement could he get the idea of space.

In advising the parent or tutor of the infant, he reminded them that memory and imagination are still inactive at the beginning of life. All that affects the child are his senses, and sensations being the primary source of knowledge, it is essential that they be presented in proper order. Since the child is attending only to his senses it behooves the tutor to show the connections of these sensations with the objects which cause them. He instructed teachers to allow the child to learn heat, cold, hardness, and softness by their sensory qualities. The child was to learn by looking, fingering, and comparing sight and touch. It is by the senses that Rousseau would educate the young child. He criticized Locke's maxim of reasoning with children. Reason is the last of the human faculties to develop and so is not the place to begin education. He insisted that children be educated first as children and then as adults. We would then be expected to teach the child at his own level of readiness and not expect to teach him that for which he has not had the necessary foundations.

The environment for the child's learning is important to Rousseau. He would have the school in the country "far from the filthy morals of the towns." The teacher is to refrain from instructing too much; it is better to set a good example and provide a suitable environment for the child to learn.

Subjects taught would be those which the child is capable of understanding and using. Modern mathematics with its reasoning requirements would never be inflicted upon a seven-year-old mind. It seems to us that children learn the things we tell them because they are able to remember and repeat what we told them. They do not understand and remember the ideas or concepts. Rousseau believed that we are prone to give children credit for having knowledge that they really do not have. It only appears so because they remember the words we say. Nothing should be taught to the child until he has the need or desire to know. Ridiculing Locke's devices, Rousseau substituted motivation.

The child would learn to read because he felt a need or desire to do so. Books would not be used, rather some kind of communication or experience charts. Rousseau believed that the order of nature was perception, memory, and reasoning. He would not expect us to inflict feats of memory and reasoning on the little brain that has not yet accomplished perception.

Intellectual reason is based on reason of the senses according to Rousseau. The senses should be the first faculties trained. The ease with which children learn is misleading to educators. Since some children seem to be able to use the senses quite well, we then assume that all children learn this sense reasoning with little or no training. Using the senses does not necessarily mean that things are perceived correctly. Refinement and discrimination of the sense organs is a necessary prerequisite to learning. Refined interaction of the senses will lead to greater ability to profit from education. Rousseau hoped for Emile to have "eyes at the end of his fingers." What was a dream for Rousseau is now a fact, as there are deaf mutes who have "ears on their feet and fingers" and can dance keeping perfect time with the orchestra.

In training the senses, Rousseau would have the child use them.

The best teacher is nature. A house would be drawn from a house, a tree from a tree and the two should be seen by the perceiver to resemble that from which they were drawn. Rousseau would not approve of modern art which is now so freely accepted in our own kindergartens where drawing is named after it is drawn. The child may never be a great artist but he will surely develop a surer hand and a finer sense of discrimination. He will at the same time be developing his visual perception. The child is not ready to learn geometry until he can draw shapes. Drawing shapes is a prerequisite to geometry.

Rousseau's first stage of mental growth or early childhood would be one of sense training and refinement of the senses. Perception must come before reason.

Johann Heinrich Pestalozzi (1746-1827)

The Swiss educator, Pestalozzi, was influenced by Rousseau's idea of a natural education for children. He, like Rousseau, attempted to write his theory by means of the story of the child's teacher. In Rousseau's case, the tutor of Emile and for Pestalozzi, the teacher, Gertrude. From his books, *Leonard and Gertrude* and *Gertrude Teaches Her Children,* we follow his ideas for educating children naturally.

For Pestalozzi, education was an experience in living, and every part of living with the children became a learning experience with a warm, kind, loving teacher who cared about all children. He preferred the informal atmosphere of natural living to that of the formal classroom. This is not to imply a totally unstructured environment because he believed that learning must be planned, graded, and structured. The child was to develop according to nature but nature was to be assisted. Pestalozzi believed that children should not be pushed to learn that for which they had not been made ready.

The *Anschauung,* or "object lesson" of Pestalozzi was based on sense impressions. By means of this *Anschauung* principle, he hoped to give man a rational conception of the world of his experience, which appeared as a sea of confused sensory perceptions. Sensory impressions were fundamental in teaching young children.

Two principles of instruction for Pestalozzi were that all learning derives from sense impression and instruction should move from the simple to the complex.

Pestalozzi believed that a child must be aware of the qualities before he could form concepts of the object as a whole. This was a sensation for Pestalozzi. Perception is based on sensation and form. To have a clear concept of objects then, it is necessary for the child to either learn its qualities accidently or deliberately.

Pestalozzi would have the child learn things according to their sequential order according to nature. A child would not learn writing until he could draw. He would first have to be able to handle and control the pencil. Before trying to draw letters, he would have to be able to draw lines and figures. These would then be drawn according to a copy, not as the child happens to want to draw them or as he may see them with distorted perception. We should insist that children copy figures, trace them, and learn their separate parts as they actually are. The child would begin by using larger letters and larger pencils refining his movements to smaller lines and figures.

The child must acquire a readiness in learning sense impressions of all kinds if he is to be able to adequately make later acquisitions of knowledge. Although Pestalozzi was primarily concerned with waifs and children of the poor, he could have been giving us instructions on teaching methods for inefficient learners when he advised that lines must be given to the child in order for him to perceive accurately. After having learned to perceive correctly, the child would then move on gradually to more abstract learnings.

Pestalozzi would instruct us in our teaching to proceed from the concrete to the abstract. In describing his method, he stresses the importance of showing the child so that he will understand before he is required to memorize.

The teacher of children according to Pestalozzi, must be a kind, gentle, loving mother who would teach by things. These would be things in the immediate environment which could be used to teach the child to see and perceive. The things would be described, discussed, and explained so that the child could understand and perceive it accurately.

The method of Pestalozzi is a plea for teachers to begin instruction at the level of the learner, use the experiences of his environment as material for learning to learn, follow an orderly sequence, and proceed from the concrete to the abstract, using the sense impressions of the learner as a base.

Jean Marc Itard (1775-1838)

The works of Itard are often mentioned by researchers interested in sensory training. He experimented with Victor, a boy of eleven or twelve, who had been found running wild in the woods. Itard had been working as a physician in an institution for deaf mutes in Paris when Victor was brought there. Victor appeared to be more animal than human. He swayed from side to side like a caged beast, bit and scratched, and showed no interest in his surroundings. Although others concluded that Victor was an incurable idiot and impossible to educate, Itard refused to accept this idea and spent four years trying to educate this boy by training the senses.

In the first series of experiments, Itard assumed that Victor was of normal intelligence and that his senses needed awakening. In this group of experiments, Itard was able to make the sense of touch, taste, and smell more responsive to stimuli, but there was no progress in sight and hearing. Color, size, and shape comparisons were used for sorting and Victor gradually acquired a relation between word and thing. Itard concluded that a different approach was necessary and without admitting that Victor might be retarded mentally to a severe degree, he did modify his method and used those more suited to an idiot.

In the second series of experiments, Itard began by concentrating on improvement of all the sense organs of this pupil. He began with the most difficult one, hearing. He attempted to isolate this sense and train it without the use of the other senses. Victor learned to discriminate between two very similar sounds and between the vowel sounds. The sounds employed became progressively less dissimilar. Itard found that this was all that could be done for this sense modality and proceeded to that of sight. Again he progressed from the greater differences to the finer discriminations and Victor learned to read and write a few words.

The sense of touch was trained next. Victor was led to feel the differences in objects, proceeding from the less similar to the more similar. Itard was pleased with the results of all of the sense training except that of hearing. In further training of the intellect, Itard found greater difficulty. Victor did learn to read a little, to write a little, and could understand others' wants from their written communications.

Although Victor became unmanageable at the onset of puberty and had to spend the remainder of his life in confinement, Itard added much to our educational methods. Many of Itard's ideas are developing into a much needed multidisciplinary approach to teaching inefficient learners, as he suggested that medicine could and should contribute to education.

Edward Sequin (1812-1880)

The continuation of the sense training theories of Itard was undertaken by his pupil, Edward Sequin. Sequin believed that his plan for educating the senses should be for all children, not just "idiots."

He was bitterly opposed to the people's school as he believed that they were more concerned with memory and allowed all other faculties to atrophy. Sequin thought that it was of utmost importance that the healthy organs be regularized and their sphere of functioning be extended. It would seem that he anticipated modern thinkers who maintain that children with learning disabilities do have some malfunctioning of the motor system. Sequin would recommend that we deal with the activity of the body before the will.

Although Itard made an attempt to isolate each sense and train it separately, Sequin believed that this was nearly impossible since the child functions as a unit. This does not imply that Sequin would begin formal education in subject matter areas before motor training had been accomplished. Sequin would begin education with motor training for all children as he believed that even the more endowed children were not as efficient in the movements of the body as they might be.

Rather than concentrate on any one defect, Sequin would treat it as part of the more general dysfunction. The body is taught to operate as an efficient unit by using each of its parts to the best advantage. The child must walk as gracefully as he possibly can. Each limb is taught to operate separately and with the whole. Sequin developed special apparatus to be used in this training. This apparatus is obviously a forerunner of our present day materials for use with children who have a disability. Pictures of it can be found in *Assistance, traitement et education des enfants, idiots et degeneres,* by Desire Magloire Bourneville, Paris, Felix Alcan, 1895.

After the child has educated the body so that it is under control of the will, he turns his attention to sensory education. Maintaining that the sense of touch is that out of which all others have developed, he begins with it. The child must handle objects and learn similarities and differences. Although Sequin stated that the senses do not operate in isolation, his method was organized so that each was deliberately taught in progressive steps.

After the sense of touch was well trained, taste and smell were the next step. In developing these senses, the differences between filth and cleanliness were also taught. The child was taught pleasant and unpleasant odors and tastes. He learned to reject filth and foul odor, which had previously been an accepted part of the life of an "idiot." In training the sense of hearing, Sequin made use of music and found it to be of great value even with the deaf.

The last sense to receive special training is the sense of sight. Sequin believed this to be the most complicated and therefore the most difficult to train. The child is taught to focus or attend to one object at a time. He is then taught to notice color, shape, size, distance, and arrangement. Although Sequin did not use the modern term "eye-hand coordination" he was describing this when he had the child use sand, then tools to draw as a prerequisite for writing.

Sequin wrote that the nature of his physiological training was not the unity of the object, but the rational comparison of objects, to be taught through any and all the senses.

PRINCIPLES OF EDUCATION FOR INEFFICIENT LEARNERS

By borrowing some of the thoughts of these earlier philosophers, who were not particularly concerned with problem learners, we could begin to form some educational principles for the education of inefficient learners. The first of these principles is that *training should begin in early childhood.*

At birth the infant has certain specialized cells which emit nervous impulses when activated outside the system. The cells of the eyes respond to light, the cells of the fingers and other areas of the body are sensitive to touch, cells in the ears are sensitive to sound, and the cells in the nose and taste buds of the tongue are sensitive to chemicals. These sense organs, which are highly specialized parts of the nervous system, enable the organism to make contact with his environment.

An individual whose sense organs are damaged, destroyed or have failed to develop is partially or totally insensitive to stimuli such as those who are blind, deaf, or perceptually handicapped as are children with learning disabilities. The sensation or activity of the sense organ must take on added meaning, characteristics, organization, significance, and experiential content before it will be a useful perception and become a tool or aid for the child's organization. Through our different perceptions we begin our learning of all things in our immediate environment. It is the way our nervous system makes contact and the organism begins to understand.

If the child is not perceiving as others perceive, he has a perceptual distortion which will continue to be distorted unless it is corrected. The early years of life then are of utmost importance in the child's development. Whether we realize it or not, the child is doing more learning than he will ever do in such a short time again. If this first learning is inaccurate, we have succeeded in allowing the child to acquire learnings that will later need to be corrected.

As far as the school is concerned, the optimum years for learning or correction of any perceptual problems are the years from kindergarten to third grade. The schools are not yet ready for the very young child, but it would seem that there is a definite need for this kind of thinking and planning if we are to prevent and correct learning problems.

A second principle for the education of inefficient learners would be to *utilize a multisensory approach*. The senses all develop simultaneously, although they develop at a different rate of speed, It would be difficult to isolate one for purposes of instruction. The motor movement of the body must be matched by visual movements such as up, down, right, and left. Poor eye-motor coordination or the ability to coordinate vision with the movements of parts of the body may result in difficulties in learning to write, cut, paste, and draw. When the hand will not do what the eye sees, the child will have many problems trying to write, bat a ball, or play games. We should then use all the senses to teach this child in order that the weak area will become strengthened.

A third principle in our educational philosophy for inefficient learners would be to *remove from the learning environment all unnecessary distractions*. The child who has an auditory discrimination handicap should not be expected to be able to improve this area if he must learn in a room filled with unnecessary noises. The noises must be shut out for him and controlled so that only those distractions which do not add to his confusion will be allowed. The addition of distractions will then be gradual and at a time when the child is ready to learn another differentiation.

The child with a visual-perceptual distortion should not be expected to be able to attend to and copy from a blackboard full of meaningless lines and spaces when he is distracted by pictures, mobiles, and other beautification programs of the teacher. His attention must be focused on that which we want him to see.

The classroom for children with learning problems should be in the most remote part of the building, away from the noise of the gymnasium, bells need not be connected to this room, and under no circumstances should the office be able to interrupt on the intercom. The windows should be high enough so that the playground is not visible to the children. If this is not possible, the bottom half of the windows can be covered with wrapping paper. Any bulletin boards that must be in the room should be at the back. The floor should be carpeted to keep the room quiet. Desk and chair should be attached to each other as the child has enough to attend to without having to keep the chair under the desk. There should be folding screens that will not fall over easily which the child may use when he wishes more privacy. All supplies are to be kept in the closets with doors on them. The child has just one thing at a time to attend to and will not be distracted by thinking of other things that are waiting for him. Even the teacher must not be a distraction. Her clothes must be calm, no jewelry, no bright colors, and she becomes as much a part of the furniture as possible.

The fourth principle applies to learning as well as discipline: *Rewards are permitted and desired, but errors are not punished.* The child who is of school age and having perceptual problems is punished enough and needs no more. He must not be punished for that which is not of his doing. This child has spent the first few years of his life being corrected for something he did not understand, now he needs to understand. Usually by the time he gets to his special teacher he has had several years of reinforced erroneous learning which must be corrected. Too often these children have been punished for dropping books off the desk when they really did not intend to do so. They just did not know where the edge of the desk stopped and the floor started.

The reward used may be a smile, praise, or some tangible reward for the younger or severely handicapped child.

Learning must begin with the concrete and then advance to the abstract is the fifth principle. We should not expect a child to be able to retain visual images correctly when he has an incorrect visual image to try to retain. We must not expect the child to utilize abilities which he does not have, or which have not been developed. The child who is expected to read at the age of seven but who cannot decide which are the letters, the black lines or the white spaces, will fail. He is not ready for these symbols and should be helped to learn them by tracing them, using letters made of sandpaper, velvet or any other means the teacher can invent.

Too often we expect children to imagine, think, and use judgment when they have not learned the basics needed to do so. We expect the child to know which number is greater when he does not know what a number is. He must work with things before symbols. The child must know what soft and hard feels like before he can give correct antonyms. It would be better to fill a gallon container than to expect a child to visualize which is larger.

We make the mistake of assuming that many of these things have been done at home or in nursery school. They may have been done before the child was capable of learning from the experience, in which case it must be repeated.

Experiences of the child in his environment provide the opportunity for learning is the sixth principle. It is in his environment that the child must function. By the time he has been placed in the special room or goes to the special teacher, he is not functioning. He is posing a problem in his behavior or his ability to learn as other children learn. He must be taught to fit in his environment and the best tool is the environment.

If the child drops everything, he must be given opportunity to learn better motor control. If the child bumps into tables and knocks them over because he does not know just where they are, he must be taught better spatial relationships. The child who cannot play baseball with the other children because he always makes outs for the team must be taught how to throw a ball, how to catch a ball, how to make a bat collide with a ball and how to run.

The things which a child cannot do in his environment are those things which he must deliberately be taught to do. The way to teach a child to play ball is to learn each of the varied skills required using the environment and materials of the environment.

In beginning to help a child with learning problems it is wise to ask the child's parents or the previous teacher to name two or three things that the child cannot do that other children his age can do. From this list just one would be chosen as the first task for this child. These are tasks from his living or learning environment. As one task is accomplished another is chosen until each of the first tasks are accomplished. A new list is then begun.

The seventh principle is probably one of the most important ones for the child with a learning problem: *teaching must begin at the instructional level of the child,* not the place or stage of development that other children his age have attained, but his own unique level. It is often necessary to return to previous stages that were not developed correctly, or perhaps not developed fully enough to provide a foundation for later learnings. This is the reason many kindergarten teachers have all the class crawling around the floor each day. They are providing for the needs of a few by inflicting it upon the group. By beginning our instruction at a level where each child can succeed consistently, we are providing for his need to believe in himself. In the beginning instruction he must have no failures, gradually a few opportunities for failure are added but in such a way that the child does not lose faith in himself. He has had many years of failing and now needs to believe he can succeed. If each new learning is preceded and followed by successes he does not lose his confidence in his own ability.

The eighth principle is too often considered to be of importance only in the primary grades: *readiness must precede instruction and the child must not be expected to learn that for which he has not been made ready.* We hear much about reading readiness in kindergarten but that is often the extent of readiness for learning in our school systems. We have one plan for readiness in kindergarten and this is for all the children, whether or not it is the kind of readiness they need. Since we cannot legally retain a child in kindergarten, the group then proceeds to first grade learnings. This practice continues throughout the grades. It is of utmost importance that we devote more attention to getting the child ready for new learning experiences at every grade level, including secondary school.

The ninth principle pertains to the teacher as well as the student: *motivation is a necessary prerequisite to learning*. The teacher must want the child to learn, and the child must be interested in learning. Most children come to kindergarten in a learning frame of mind. That is, they really are interested in learning when they begin their career in school. For the inefficient learner, who does not quite fit the mold or pattern the teacher has laid out for the group, this motivation or desire is damaged in a very short time.

It is a very difficult task to try to teach a child something that he does not want to learn, or is unable to learn by the method we have chosen. It is not so difficult to help a child learn, once we have determined what the problem in learning happens to be. It would seem feasible to find this problem as early as possible before all desire to learn has been destroyed or compounded with emotional problems caused by the inability to function as others do. Those few children who appear to have no desire to learn must be helped to want to learn. For each child the method may be different and the wise teacher will learn from the child which method is best suited to the individual child.

The tenth principle concerns the teacher of the inefficient learners: *the teachers must be able to establish rapport with any child and must provide a learning environment which fits his needs*. Although no two experts seem to agree on the qualifications for a good teacher, or can define a good teacher, they do agree that the teacher must like and respect children and the children must like and respect the teacher. This situation does not often come about accidentally, particularly with children who have been creating problems since infancy and have learned to be disliked by the time they arrive at school. The teacher must find something to like, which is really not as difficult as it may appear.

These children have one thing in common, their ability to function efficiently as an individual in spite of a handicap. This alone should earn them our respect and attention. With the necessary educational foundations as a background, the teacher is then able to learn from the child how best to help him learn. This should not be camouflaged or hidden from the child. He needs to know that he has at last found someone who will help or try to help him. This is not to imply a permissive atmosphere. More often there is little of a permissive atmosphere. The difference is that the child knows and understands that this is done to help him and not as punishment. He knows that there are times when he needs to be restrained and he appreciates restraint until he can be helped to do it for himself. This teacher, like Pestalozzi's Gertrude, must be all things to all children.

Some current theories of child development which appear to be based on these educational principles will be reviewed in Chapter III.

Chapter III

A PSYCHOLOGICAL BASIS FOR SENSE TRAINING

FRANCES MARLING

THE DEVELOPMENTAL THEORY OF JEAN PIAGET

THE THEORIES of Jean Piaget regarding child development have once again been revived in the United States. His description of cognitive development is pertinent and momentous for the schools of the 1960's.

Piaget's approach to the study of child development reflects his biological background since he conveys two evolutionary aspects in his theories: (1) There is a continuous fitting of old structures into new functions under changed circumstances. (2) These adaptations do not develop in isolation.

The bulk of Piaget's scientific data is concerned mainly with the structural aspect of the intellect, understanding the thinking processes of the child at particular periods of his life, and the differences among the various ages.

Piaget's cognitive theory is concerned with the intellectual life of the child. He believes that there are definite and regular patterns in cognitive development. Since these patterns are experienced by everyone, we should be able to predict an individual's range of comprehension according to the sequential patterns. Piaget's theory describes intelligence and learning as active, not passive, constantly acquiring new actions and organizing them into operational groupings. These organizational activities within the individual are acting upon the environment rather than the environmental cues stimulating the individual.

Intellectual activity is an active process of adapting the new to the old while retaining the old. Each new learning modifies the old, and there is a definite organizational pattern.

The organizational patterns which are interrelated reflect a definite sequence. Although ages are approximated, the degree and rate of development is completely individual.

The theories and philosophy of Piaget basically rest on his inherent respect for human life. The cycle of birth, life, and growth creates a sense of awe and he strongly feels the human worth and dignity of the individual. He believed that each individual is unique and possesses a wide range of potentialities.

Intellectual Development

Piaget described his theory of intellectual development as evolving through various stages. He viewed all development as proceeding through a continuous process of generalization differentiation. There are regular patterns in cognitive development and they are experienced by everyone. He looked upon development as an inherent unalterable evolutional process; yet within this developmental process he located a series of distinct phases and subphases. This process is organized and integrative and all other areas of development are interrelated with intellectual development. He tried to identify the structures of each age level and to show how they adapt to and modify environmental demands. Piaget established that intellectual development follows a predictable pattern toward maturity. Developmental phases are consistently ordered and follow five distinct stages. There is a difference between child and adult behavior. Mature behavior originates in infant behavior and follows a definite pattern. Maturity is realized when all stages are integrated.

Intelligence is a process of adaptation and organization. Adaption consists of mutually interrelated cooperative features—assimilation and accommodation. The biological term *assimilation* merely means the organism is able to handle or cope with the situation presented to it. *Accommodation* is the ability to change in order to adapt or adjust. Due to this accommodation process and his unique stage of readiness, the child must constantly be reevaluating his perception of his environment. As he adjusts to new stages, so he adjusts his perception. Assimilation and accommodation are a part of the complete experience and an object needs this process for total involvement. Instrumental in the child's system of ordering is the schema. It serves as a mediator between assimilation and accommodation. The schema is the organization of the child's past and existing experience in his environment. Piaget defined schemas as essentially repeatable psychological units of intelligent action. They may be described as types of plans that the individual has at his disposal when interacting with the environment.

According to Piaget, the cognitive schema and the sensorimotor schema are similar and totally interrelated. One is dependent upon the other for the cognitive processes of internalization, cognitive schema develops from sensorimotor schema.

In his book, *The Psychology of Intelligence,* Piaget stated that intelligence is not an isolated and sharply differentiated class of cognitive processes. Rather it is a form of equilibrium toward which cognitive and motor adaptation tend.

Stages of Development

The Sensorimotor Stage (0-2 years)

Piaget considers this stage to be of utmost importance because this is the foundation on which more complex conceptual schemas develop.

The infant organizes sensory information. Though it is adaptive behavior, initial cognitive and conceptual designs are not yet apparent. This adaptive and intelligent infant behavior and the sensorimotor schemas are the roots out of which later conceptual schemas develop. Through sequential repetition, the experience stimulus becomes a signal value and reactions become closely linked with the stimulus. Piaget described sensorimotor intelligence as the coordination of successive overt movements without fusion and continuous vision necessary for understanding the whole. It is beneficial to repeat that the cognitive schemas derive from sensorimotor schemas by process of internalization. Once achieved, this development in turn stimulates new processes of human behavior. Most roots for future cognitive understanding are acquired during this important sensorimotor stage.

Preoperational Stage (2-7 years)

This stage is further divided into two substages: preconceptual thought and intuitive thought.

Piaget views preconceptual thought as the beginning of conceptual thought. The child is beginning to use language as a conveyor of meaning rather than using actions. The child at this point is in a state of disequilibrium in his conceptual thinking. He thinks others see the world as he does—egocentric. He makes no distinction between the general and the particular.

By four years of age, the child is entering into the last phase of the preoperational stage, intuitive thought. He is beginning to act in a consistent pattern of reasoning. One significant aspect that should not be overlooked is that the child experiences difficulty in maintaining and considering two ideas concurrently. Also, the child is still unable to relate the parts to the whole for he becomes preoccupied with its parts. Thinking in terms of the whole is perplexing and uncertain.

During the intuitive stage the child is able to compare and identify two sets of objects or a series of ideas if placed consecutively. But if the objects or ideas are scattered in a different sequence it may not yet be possible for the child to rearrange them in their original order.

Operational Stage (7-16 years)

Concrete operations (7-11 years) and formal operational thought (11-16 years) are two substages. The child's thoughts are beginning to stabilize and the process of assimilation and accommodation are no longer "pulling." A higher state of equilibrium exists. Piaget calls the operational structures between the ages of seven and eleven "concrete" because their starting point is always some real system of objects and relations that the child perceives; that is, the operations are carried out on concrete objects. The child reaches an organizational understanding of the concrete object in his environment.

During the last substage (formal operational thought) the child becomes a youth who is able to relate concrete and abstract objects to one another. He sees the world as it is now and what it possibly could be.

Piaget's theory of child development is a dramatic unfolding of action and growth proceeding from the simple towards the complex, concrete to abstract, general to the specific, and from infancy to adulthood. His contributions to educators are poignant and noteworthy.

It is highly advantageous for the teacher of disadvantaged children to study and interpret Piaget's theories of child development. The child is not a miniature adult. Piaget reminds us that there is absolute continuity of developmental patterns and each level or cycle finds its roots in the former phase. The developmental sequence therefore does not omit stages or progress in a haphazard manner. Since development proceeds according to these sequential patterns, the child structures his world quite differently than does the adult.

THE DEVELOPMENTAL THEORY OF ARNOLD GESELL

Growth is the key concept in Gesell's theory of child development. The growth cycle is perpetual and successive from the day of conception through adulthood. Uniquely one, the body and mind progress and mature through the organizing process of growth. Gesell reminded us that developmental research of growth should be studied on a comparative basis. Though all children proceed through definite sequential patterns, it must be interpreted in relative terms. No two children grow exactly the same way. Each child has his own individual style of growth which might be determined by inheritance. The emphasis is upon individual differences.

The rate of development during the first five years is phenomenal. It proceeds in a spiraling, integrative manner. Gesell described it as fluid and continuous. The maturational process which brings growth to a state of completeness remains the same throughout the whole life cycle. There is a constant building and interweaving of an infinite pattern and subpattern.

The developmental process during the period from five to ten years is not as dramatic nor as prodigious. Behavioral pattern changes are more subtle and sometimes obscured by the pleasures of home and school activity. Because of this dilemma, often educators as well as parents dismiss the ways of the growing child. Lack of knowledge or understanding that the child is not yet completely matured leads to possible maladjustment.

Deeper understanding of the developmental process of the individual child from five years to ten years will foster more meaningful communication between child and adult. A grave mistake is made if educators and parents overlook the differences in growth and maturation in the individual child.

Gesell's maturity trait profiles of the school child are briefly described as follows:

Age Five

For this brief period the child enjoys a phase of balance. Soon the push of growth and cultural demands create an imbalance and the child moves from five to six years. The five-year-old enjoys a routine and adjusts well to an activity program which allows freedom of movement and yet maintains control of the sequence of separate activities. Most of the time he completes one activity before doing another. His sense of time is concerned chiefly with **now**. It is difficult for him to conceive of himself as not having existed or as dying. Time for him is largely his own personal time. The five-year-old's spatial interest is in what is here. He is extremely focal and is interested in the space which he immediately occupies. He has little insight into geographic relationships, but does recognize some specific landmarks.

Age Six

The six-year-old child is less integrated. He has not fully found either himself or his environment. The child experiences many tensions and is somewhat impulsive, undifferentiated, compulsive, and excitable. It is interesting to note that Gesell strongly believes that the six-year-old is still not ready for all-day attendance. The six-year-old is oriented to the whole room and is constantly on the move or manipulating things. He becomes impatient when his flow of movement is interrupted. The six-year-old will vascillate between two choices. He does not live as much in the **now** as did the five-year-old. He wants to recapture time past, and shows marked interest in hearing about his own babyhood. Duration of an episode in time has little meaning for him. His spatial concepts like so many others are relatively undifferentiated.

Age Seven

The child at this age now has himself more under control. He has a greater capacity to absorb and organize his new cultural experiences, and establishes more firm relationships with his peers. Day by day he grows in mental stature becoming aware not only of himself, but of others. He is more reflective and takes time to think. His mental life is embracing the community and also the cosmos. He has a more intelligent awareness of the sun, moon, and clouds, heat, fire, and the earth's crust. His orientation of time and space is improving and he can associate a specific time with a specific task.

Age Eight

The eight-year-old has built a firmer body of experiences that enable him to give as well as take. There is more initiative and spontaneity in meeting his environment and he is seeking deeper orientation in time and space. At eight the child begins to see conclusions, contexts and implications which before he had seen only in part. The universe is less disconnected for him and he begins to see himself more clearly as a person among persons, acting, participating, and enjoying.

Age Nine

This age indicates more awareness to his surroundings and much more dependency. A nine-year-old is able to summon reserves of energy and renew his attack for repeated trials. This is due to the greater maturity of his whole behavioral equipment. He is ready to undertake any task that is reasonably within his grasp. He has greater interest in process and skill and is more able to analyze his movements, both before and during action. At nine the child's individuality seeks to reassert and to reorganize itself. He is engaged in mastering skills.

Age Ten

The child is now able to attend to a visual task and yet maintain conversation. He is now more receptive and fluid. He is capable in carrying on elementary discussions of social problems. The ten-year-old shows a genuine capacity to budget his time and energy. His general behavior, his demeanors, and his orientation to the household are more modulated. The ten-year-old is in good equilibrium and his individuality is now well defined. His insights are so much more mature that we can see an adult in the making.

Gesell is very thorough in his comparative research dealing with the stages of child development. His developmental patterns are easy to follow and interpret. Comprehensive profiles of a child at a certain stage of growth serve as a very helpful resource manual. Sincere effort on the part of Arnold Gesell has been made to inform and educate people who manage and teach children. If adults make a habit of thinking in terms of the growth sequences and what can be expected of a child at the certain stages, the child is more apt to possess sound mental maturity.

APPLICATION OF THEORY TO EDUCATIONAL PLANNING

Though major school objectives are the same for all children, the inefficient learner will benefit from a program with certain modifications. Is it possible that if Piaget and Gesell's theories were put into practice from the beginning, the population of children with learning problems would be at a bare minimum?

Piaget and Gesell's theory of sequential growth pattern is most applicable when planning a curriculum. For example, expecting a child to find contextual clues at the age of seven will only confuse him. Before the child is able to engage in abstract verbal interaction (eleven to twelve years) he should first be active and discovering by manipulating objects.

By allowing the child to regulate his own rate of learning rather than the teacher imposing upon him what she think should be learned, he may then gain confidence through success, and no longer be in need of remedial treatment.

Before listing specific objectives of the program, it is beneficial to review Piaget and Gesell's theories concerning child development:

1. Each child develops at his own rate of speed and no two children progress alike. Not all are ready at the same time to master the same skills.

2. Time and space orientation develop very slowly throughout the ages five to eleven.

3. Conceptual thought begins around eleven years of age.

4. Development must follow a sequential pattern in normal progression and the child structures his thinking and world differently than does the adult.

5. The six-year old is still not ready for all-day attendance—rest periods are beneficial.

6. Physical development precedes intellectual development and both are interrelated.

7. Children experience tension and pressures for they are constantly seeking to understand and evaluate their world about them.

8. At the age of seven and eight the child is still mastering skills.

9. At seven and eight the child cannot maintain two ideas simultaneously. They are still preoccupied with the parts of the whole.

Specific objectives for a program of remediation for inefficient learners on the basis of Piaget's and Gesell's theories of development are the following:

1. To develop an objective screening program for the identification of disadvantaged learners in kindergarten and primary grades.

2. To demonstrate the adaptation of individualized and prescriptive teaching techniques.

3. To start where the child is and structure and sequence subject matter for a more effective learning experience.

4. To set up a specific sensorimotor training program for those children whose senses need refinement.

5. To set up a specific physical education program for children whose motor coordination is not fully developed.

6. To help the child master skills through the process of demonstration, exercise, repetition, and reinforcement. Behavior and intellectual patterns are established from previous experiences, starting at the level of each individual child and adding successful experiences is important. Verbal teaching methods according to Piaget should begin about age eleven and twelve. Most of the experiences prior to this age should be activity, interaction, and manipulation.

7. To help children master basic skills in a sequential manner for continuous progress of intellectual development.

8. To promote adjustment in social and emotional development.

9. The diagnostic team will follow a curriculum guide that is flexible and adaptable for each child's prescription.

10. To use a multisensory approach to all learning.

11. To use special class time for fine muscular development activity, for writing, and manipulating objects.

12. To broaden the child's background of experience.

Chapter IV

TWENTIETH CENTURY THEORIES OF EDUCATIONAL METHODS FOR INEFFICIENT LEARNERS

Maria Montessori (1870-1952)

MARIA MONTESSORI was one of the twentieth century theorists in educational methods whose plan for teaching stressed the sense experience reminiscent of Pestalozzi, Itard, and Sequin.

Early in the twentieth century Maria Montessori, the first woman to receive a Doctor of Medicine degree from the University of Rome, showed the influence of these earlier theorists in the development of didactic materials for the education of retarded children. Although her method had many other implications, sense training is a basic consideration.

Montessori established a prepared environment in which the children were free to use materials. Each was to be used in a specific manner and each provided a portion of the self-education that Montessori envisioned. The materials provided experience with length, breadth, height, color, texture, weight, size, and form. She considered sense training to be a prerequisite to higher intellectual functioning. Montessori became a pupil and studied the attempts of experimental psychology of Itard, the famous French physician, and the materials of Sequin, his disciple. No one before Montessori's time had produced a system in experimental pedagogy. She initiated a plan of teaching that enabled many abnormal children to reach grade level.

In January, 1907, she established the first school in Via dei Masi and christened it Casa Dei Bambini, or Children's House. Her acceptance of this commission was partly swayed by the desire to try her principles on normal children. Another wish was to make this a school for scientific experimental pedagogy and child psychology.

Like Comenius, her training procedures were sequences of experience carefully constructed to proceed from the concrete to the abstract, in order to develop mental concepts which would naturally lead to the language arts and verbal skills. The emphasis was on self-correcting materials. When a child replaced a form in the form board, he matched that form in its proper place. He was able to separate figure from ground. His hands confirmed what his eyes had perceived. He corrected his own mistakes, and this information was securely stored for future use.

In Children's House an environment was created that offered opportunity to enhance social growth for a child. Furniture was scaled to size. It was a real house for children. In the central room was the room for intellectual work which contained the didactic work for intellectual training.

In spite of social prejudice and bigotry, Maria Montessori became the first woman upon whom the University of Rome conferred the degree of Doctor of Medicine. Her first step into educational fields was as Assistant Doctor in the Psychiatric Clinic of the University of Rome, and this necessitated many trips into the slums to obtain subjects.

Mental and social deprivation of children in the slum areas aroused the maternal sympathy of Montessori. She became convinced that mentally defective slum children could be aided by means of systematized methods of teaching and discipline. As a result of Montessori's insistence upon the value of these theories, the State Orthophrenic School was established with her at its head.

Teachers were trained by Montessori for this experimental approach. Training of these educators was directed to open their minds and hearts to an awareness of the "natural phenomena" of a child's revelation from a prepared experiment. Techniques in the proper use of hand and arm muscles were required for success in the use of the teaching instruments.

A reward to a child was in the mastery of a new learning experience. Faliure was to be quietly overlooked.

Teaching was practically individualized. Speaking was maintained at a minimum to avoid confusion and distraction. Directions were brief, simple, and objective. Teachers were almost observers as they seldom explained and rarely guided.

Materials used for didactic work in the education of the senses consisted of sets of solid insets, sets of solids in graduated sizes, cubes, prisms, rods, tablets of rough and smooth surfaces, boxes of things to touch, tablets of different weights, cards with pasted geometric forms, closed boxes for sounds, musical balls, materials for writing and arithmetic, sticks for counting, colored pencils, frames for buttoning, and colored boxes containing colored spools.

Montessori, like Locke, recognized the value of utilizing play activities as a tool for learning. These materials that seemed like play were actually designed for particular purposes. It is by experimentation and manipulation that a young child is able to perfect his sensory motor data and is able to orient himself in space. The child must educate himself through the use of carefully selected materials.

Montessori's method is divided into three parts. Motor education, she believed, would be accommodated by the care and management of the environment. Sensory education of language would be provided for in her didactic materials.

Motor education was an exploration of the environment to coordinate movements and also by touching things. Any physical activities in the management of their little household, gardening, and care of their persons were to be considered part of motor activity. One type of gymnastic exercise was to walk a painted line on the floor much as a tightrope walker, with no danger of falling. Music was played occasionally in the form of a march. There was, however, little rhythmic work, gesture songs, or dramatic play for imagination and self-expression.

Sensory education was a definite part of the Montessori method. One type of sensory approach using the didactic materials was the wooden cylinders with little buttons for handles. The first set contained round cylinders of the same height, but the diameters increased in size from thick to thin. They were to be placed in round holes in a long box. Each cylinder had an exact place in the box. The second set had wooden cylinders that decreased both in width and height. The last set of cylinders were of the same diameter but decreased in height.

The child sat in a comfortable position and quietly mixed the cylinders and then held the button of one cylinder while attempting to find its correct place in the box. The child was to learn by doing.

His errors are obvious to him and his successes are immediately rewarded.

During the motor education activities and the sensory education, language development was initiated. While the child was working with the cylinders, the instructor would hand the child a cylinder saying, "This is thick." The child would associate the cylinder by manipulation and know it to be thick. The same procedure was used with a thin cylinder. The instructor would then ask the child for the thick cylinder or for the thin one to test receptive language. This was followed by expressive language as the instructor would ask the child, "What is thick?"

Montessori, by means of simple didactic self-correcting self-teaching materials, employed a multisensory approach to the senses and initiated speech and language development.

Tactile education was considered of extreme importance and was taught in a specific manner. The child was taught to suspend his hand and very lightly with his fingertips glide over the surface of varied materials in a left to right direction as in writing. The board was divided in half, with one side of sandpaper and the other side a smooth surface. Later materials and then objects were used, and with eyes closed the children were encouraged to make a systematic search of the materials.

Concepts were learned through the use of concrete materials. Only one sense was trained at a time. This was to eliminate confusion and establish mental order. As an example, the color tablets that were used were uniform in size and weight, only the color was different. There were eight shades of each color. The number of tablets was gradually increased. Beginning with a few strongly contrasting stimuli, the children progressed to many stimuli of gradual differentiation.

Education of the senses was accomplished by repetition. The intent was not to know colors, qualities or forms, but rather for a refinement of the senses in making comparisons, judgments, and for exercise of the intellect.

Language was initiated during the motor and sensory training periods. More deliberately formal procedures were later used.

The children traced around small inserts with colored pencils. When the inserts were removed, the children filled them in with strokes and later with parallel lines as the first step toward writing.

In reading, as in writing, parts were learned and then associated with wholes. This approach emphasized the alphabet, sounding of letters, particularly in combinations, observing the letter in writing, and noting it in printed form.

Letters of the alphabet were cut from wood in script form. Montessori later discovered that a paper alphabet was easily manipulated and produced the same results. Consonants were blue enameled onto wooden letters, and the vowels were painted red.

It appears that another person with an educator's point of view had conceived the idea of a manipulatable alphabet prior to Montessori. In AD 403, St. Jerome wrote to Laeta, "Get her a set of letters made of boxwood or ivory and call each by its proper name. Let her play with these, so that even her play may teach her something."

The paper alphabet letters could be placed on cards that had the same color and shape of the wooden alphabet. The cards could be constructed of sandpaper with a picture that corresponds to an object beginning with that letter.

Above this letter shape was printed a large letter in script and a small one in printed form. The children followed the form of the letter with one finger and then traced it with the index and middle finger to fix muscular memory for writing. Learning and work retention were aided by the tracing and writing of the word. This was followed by the use of a wooden stick held as a pencil to follow the design. Montessori conceived the idea of a furrow in the wooden alphabet to follow the form of letter, but due to the expense of this project, the idea never materialized.

Three steps were used to teach letters. A letter was introduced with its phonetic sound as "This is *a*." This associated the letter name and encouraged the use of the visual, tactile, and muscular senses. Next, the teacher would request a letter by using the phonetic sound. The last step would be to ask the child, "What is this?" This checked the child for recognition and sound as well as language development.

Words were sounded out letter by letter as viewed with cards. The teacher would say, "Faster," as the child said each letter in the words. She would repeat this until the child suddenly heard all the sounds together and recognized the word.

Visitors to the Children's Houses never failed to be impressed with the "lesson of silence." It began as a lesson for the sense of hearing and turned into a game that the children dearly loved. Children from lower socioeconomic groups, due to crowded conditions, are not as capable of distinguishing the relevant from irrelevant sounds. They find it equally difficult to listen to directions and are not as ready for group testing.

This is a "no-nonsense classroom" and a "prepared environment" of self-correcting "didactic apparatus." The directress continues her role of background observer and comes to the foreground only when necessary to prepare another lesson, guide, or encourage.

Upon the foundations established by Itard and Sequin, Montessori built a plan of teaching which reflects the thinking of Comenius, Locke, Rousseau, and Pestallozzi. She made use of a multisensory approach, she expected a controlled environment, distractions were reduced, success was provided, and she recognized the necessity of early training.

Alfred Strauss and Laura Lehtinen

The work of Alfred Strauss and Laura Lehtinen, *Psychopathology and Education of the Brain-Injured Child,* has become a classic work concerning the minimally brain-injured child. Its initial presentation was so basic in scope in the teaching approach that authorities in this field frequently refer to it.

Through experimental psychological investigations and clinical observations, it was realized that a special educative process was needed for these children. Whether motor areas were damaged or intact, in all instances there was damage to the central nervous system.

To avoid distractibility of stimulus to the brain-injured child, the classroom setting was drastically altered. Groupings of children were small with twelve as a maximum. Walls were painted in subdued colors. Bulletin boards and pictures were kept at a minimum. If a second floor classroom could not be utilized, the first floor windows were partially covered with paper. Children's desks were turned to face the wall, and screens were placed around the more hyperactive children. This seems to be an application of Comenius' desire to remove distractions.

Reading readiness for the brain-injured child is not as readily determinable as for the normal child. Discrepancies in the visual and auditory modalities may vary as well as maturity and emotional factors.

Strauss and Lehtinen believed that the teaching goal for the brain-injured could be accomplished by systematically arranging experiences rather than waiting for cumulative readiness indicators. They also felt that with some modifications remedial work could follow approximately the same principles as they had established for the child who had never learned to read.

Initially, their program began with the development of visual perception which was intended as a means to form parts into a whole, provide experiences with forms, and to organize space. Puzzles were the mediae used, much as Locke would have used games. Simple pictures were cut into two parts and assembled. Several sections were then marked with heavy crayon, and the picture puzzle was cut and assembled. Progression from the simple to the complex was intended as preparation for the use of commercial puzzles. In the event this proved too difficult, a figure of a person or an animal was cut into two pieces for assembling.

Simple geometric designs were drawn on cards and matched. Color cues were added to significant parts of the more complex designs. A cardboard tachistoscope was assembled to expose one design at a time while another child searched for a similar shape. Exercises with geometric shapes were intended as preparation for alphabet work.

Children made their own alphabet cards and matched similar letters. To assist in directional placement of the letters, color cues were used. Letters from cards were cut into two parts as a puzzle and then matched for further structuralization. At this point whole words were matched for form and only their meaning explained. Handwriting was introduced very early and considered to be very important and an essential factor in the development of reading readiness.

Future independence in word recognition was structured by means of auditory and perceptual analysis. Letters have shapes but represent sounds as well. For brain-injured children particular guidance was essential to properly analyze and discriminate each sound to the whole word, thus organizing the Gestalt.

Phonics training was initially focused on oral or sound interpretation alone. Letter symbols and pictures came later. Vowels were introduced from familiar words, the particular sound was made known, and then it was reproduced in isolation. Vowel sounds being inconsistent were color-cued to provide an association between the color and sound. Consonants that were easily recognized visually as well as auditorily were taught first. Caution was exercised in producing clear letter sounds when voiced in isolation.

Visual symbols were introduced after auditory discrimination was reasonably established. Writing reinforced this association. Magazine and newspaper hunts were made for the letters of specified sounds and pasted on cards. Picture cards were matched with letter symbols.

Words were built by copying on cards, writing papers, and with stamping sets. Color cues were used to emphasize predominant features of consonants, written on the blackboards, or built with letter cards as the teacher spoke the word separating each sound. In beginning reading, an analytical method rather than the global approach was preferred. Word study, therefore, was an important part of the readiness program. Early reading was structured for an intellectual approach, not as a memory exercise for the brain-injured.

Formal reading began after the acquisition of ten or more words that would appear in the reading. These words were presented in context in various ways as simple phrases, labels, or sentences to check comprehension.

Distractibility occured frequently during beginning reading. Markers and fingers were used to denote the foreground word against the confusion of background words. Another technique was a piece of heavy paper with a slotted middle section which allowed for a one-line exposure. To limit disinhibition, color cues were often used. Another procedure was to cut workbooks into sentences or compose individual sentences.

New words were written, studied, written in stories or sentences and then dictated to the children. This forced integration of phonics knowledge.

Auditory-visual relationships were strengthened by oral reading. Oral reading provided the brain-injured child with personal confidence and satisfaction from the auditory stimuli and motor components of speech. He enjoyed his own voice as well as the voices of the other children. This enjoyment extended over a longer period than it would have for the intact child. Children were encouraged to read their lessons in soft voices while at their desks. When reading speed and distractibility could be controlled, only then was silent reading emphasized.

Disturbances in auditory perception of the brain-injured children, however, soon became apparent to Strauss and Lehtinen, particularly if children relied exclusively on visual interpretation. Children were unsure in their differentiation of isolated sounds and reproduced them only with the greatest difficulty. Inaccurate spatial organization of sounds caused inability to pronounce a word in proper auditory sequence, for example, "aminal" for "animal" and "bakset" for "basket." Dissection of a word into sounds or the construction of sounds into words was arduous and even impossible for many of the children. Rhyming in free association was not possible in far too many cases.

Initial procedures and development of their reading program was commenced due to immediate educative needs of the brain-injured children. The approach was an attack on organic disturbances and not intended as a psychotherapeutic means of relieving emotional conflicts, increasing interest or furnishing motivation.

Learning to read requires an understanding and application of the English language. Perception is related to language, and anything that distorts or retards perception will also delay language. Knowledge of word meaning and visual imagery of their shapes are only part of success in reading. Skill in decoding the visual images into auditory-verbal units must follow. If a childs auditory-perceptual organization can be compared accurately with his visual-perceptual one, he has established basic reading skills. Inference here is that he knows the word meaning, phonetic characteristics, the word form, temporal sequencing of the word sounds, and that he can correctly interpret it with the proper vocal sequential utterance. Brain-injured children are either limited or untrained in their ability to organize the stimuli coming in to transfer symbols for use into a means of communication. They must then be taught or trained to do those things which other children seem to learn accidentally.

The method of Strauss and Lehtinen seems to reflect some of the principles of earlier thinkers. They, like Comenius, believed in early childhood education. They seem to have followed the ten rules Comenius listed in summing up his principles. Education is to begin early, it is to proceed from the easy to the difficult, nothing is to be presented until the mind is ready for it, progress is to be slow, and a multi-sensory approach is to be utilized.

Like Rousseau, Comenius and Pestallozzi, Strauss and Lehtinen are concerned about the environment of the school and would prefer a quiet location, free from distraction.

MODERN ADVOCATES OF SENSORIMOTOR ACTIVITIES AS A KEY TO LEARNING

The new theorists in education of inefficient learners who believe that the sensorimotor system should function efficiently in order for perceptual learning to take place might well be called the Strauss-Lehtinen-Kephart school of thought, as these researchers all emphasize the importance of sensorimotor skills in the training of children with learning problems. This is an extension of the work begun originally by Strauss and his associates with the classical brain-injured child. As such, it represents an extension of the earlier philosophy to encompass a much larger group of children who come to school and manifest learning and behavioral disorders.

These new writers are agreed that there is a need for social competence, vocational training, emotional health, and academic training. They also seem to agree that certain preparation is essential before any of these areas can be dealt with effectively in the classroom. Two of the preparations to which they continually refer are the following: a) the motor system must function efficiently, and b) sense modalities are a foundation upon which is built the forms of higher intellectual functioning.

Newell C. Kephart

Newell C. Kephart was a student of Alfred E. Strauss and later was co-author of one of the texts to which most modern writers refer when discussing the brain-injured child and his education. Kephart was director of the Achievement Center for Children at Purdue University until 1968 when he moved to Colorado to provide the same type of services for children and teachers. Not only is he working with children, but he also works with their parents and with future teachers. His best known book is *The Slow Learner in the*

Classroom, although his many pamphlets and speeches have been most useful in adapting his methods to many problem learners with a surprising degree of success.

Newell Kephart seems to be echoing Maria Montessori in emphasizing the importance of perceptual motor match. He feels that there is a significant interrelationship between motor activities which are initially of a gross, exploratory nature in early childhood and perceptual skill of later developmental years. He says that through this process of perceptual-motor matching, perceptual data comes to supply the same consistent body of information that earlier motor data supplies. He believes that the child perfects the sensorimotor processes by the manipulation of things and by manipulating his body in relation to things.

Kephart discussed the necessity for providing specifically designed exercises for developing perceptual-motor matching. He says that civilization is making increased demands for finer and more specific discriminations in the perceptual areas and at the same time by its very nature is decreasing the opportunity offered to develop the skills to make these fine discriminations by offering less opportunity to children to explore the world in terms of multiple and varied experiences. He feels that massive amounts of experimentation and experience are necessary in order for children to develop refined abilities in the area of perceptual discrimination, which Kephart feels, has its beginnings in sensorimotor discriminations that are made in early childhood.

Kephart felt that the motor pattern lies at the basis for all additional learning. Therefore, where the motor pattern is faulty, the higher order of learnings will be similarly faulty. The foundation must be laid first and well established before the superstructure can be raised. Only in this way can we be assured that the whole will be sound. At the Achievement Center for Children, therapy begins with motor training. Only after the motor generalization begins to develop is the child placed in perceptual or academic training.

The Perceptual-Motor Survey which has been developed by Kephart consists of ten areas to be examined and rated. These are as follows: a) performance on a walking board, b) jumping tasks, c) identification of body parts, d) imitation of movements, e) obstacle course, f) angels in the snow, g) stepping stones, h) chalkboard, i) ocular pursuits, and j) visual achievement forms. If there are deficits in any of these areas, Kephart gives suggested training activities to use in correcting the deficit.

An adaption of this survey and the accompanying training exercises have been developed with Dr. Kephart's assistance by Dr. Glenn Lowder at Winter Haven, Florida.

The Winter Haven Program

The old adage "nothing succeeds like success" is one of the basic underlying principles of the Winter Haven Lions Research Foundation Perceptual Training and Testing Program.

About fifteen years ago, a group in Winter Haven, Florida, was aroused after hearing a speaker on the then currently popular theme, "Why Johnny Can't Read." The group, the local Lions Club, decided to appoint a committee to determine if something could be done to help the many children that were experiencing difficulty in their school work. These children had to be found before they could be helped. A ten-man committee attempted to find a test which might predict some of the possible failures so that these children could be given additional help before they had become serious reading problems.

The committee sought the aid of local first grade teachers, vision specialists, psychologists, other educators, and much technical literature in determining the type of test which would be most useful. The information suggested that the test should not be time consuming, be simple to administer, have a reliable scoring scale and be nonverbal.

With these four ideas in mind, the committee found its research pointing to geometric forms as a possibility for such a test. They looked into the work of Dr. Arnold Gesell at Yale University's Child Development Clinic. There, a test had been standardized to determine the visual maturation of children under nine years of age. After a full year of research in the area, the committee recommended that the club finance further research in the field. The research was undertaken to determine if Gesell's forms could detect future reading problems when used in the regular classroom rather than in the clinical situation.

The forms were tried on 1,500 school children in the areas and the results showed a marked contrast between good and poor readers.

When Dr. Kephart became interested in the project he recommended and supervised a graduate study to analyze the extensive records which had been collected by the Lions Club Committee. He appointed Dr. Robert Glenn Lowder, then a graduate student, to analyze the tests. The resultant doctoral thesis, *Perceptual Ability and School Achievement,* definitely confirmed the test's value.

As a result of this study, Dr. Lowder proposed several questions. He asked if training on the forms might not improve reading skills. He felt that since outline form perception seemed to be learned and developmental, perhaps systematic perceptual training might result in improved reading achievement.

The Lions Club found that form templates had long been used as a standard training device for retarded and neurologically impaired children. They theorized that the tactile and kinesthetic reinforcement supplied by the template might help the child having perceptual difficulty to learn the various geometric forms.

For the retarded children, these templates represented an effective means of assisting them in building better directional control for their sensorimotor activities, especially at their directional visual-motor near-at-hand school tasks. For the child of average ability, however, the templates represented an aid in improving perception of forms which are incorporated in the letters and words a child must perceive and remember accurately for successful reading.

As the program grew and further research produced positive results, the amateur committee of researchers sought professional guidance. They formed the Winter Haven Lions Research Foundation and appointed an advisory board of educators, psychologists, engineers, medical men, and vision specialists. The chairman of the advisory board is Dr. Emmet A. Betts, an authority in reading and a research professor at the University of Miami. One of the men most closely associated with the organization is Dr. Charles McQuarrie, a Winter Haven optometrist, who is the executive director of the Research Foundation.

From its beginning as a group testing program to be easily employed by the classroom teacher, the Winter Haven Program has grown to the point where it now includes rythmic training, posture exercises, balancing and coordination drills, as well as the original drawing and manipulation of the various geometric forms. The program thus involves sensorimotor and perceptual motor training.

The program, which involves the body as well as the mind, is basically a nonverbal prereading method which employs geometric targets and form templates as part of the teaching and training procedures used with children who are not reaching expected levels. It is not a program that replaces the normal classroom curriculum but is used in addition to, and before, formal teaching of reading is begun.

The development of effective visual perception is the main concern of the Winter Haven Program. Through the use of the templates, the kindergarten and first grade children learn to draw the various geometric designs, thus increasing their ability to recognize form contour and to differentiate between the angles of a square and those of a diamond. The training lets the children better understand the actual size of the perceived objects. It gives them a better awareness of contour, boundaries of the forms, spatial relationships, and a kinesthetic feel of the various figures.

It has been found that within six weeks, distortions shown in the original drawings of the slower students in a class will often be eliminated. Children show increased maturity, learn faster, and do better than children in a control group. The most dramatic effect seems to be in the area of reading. It seems that the result of training increases the awareness of form and shape and would therefore have a pronounced effect on the child's ability to better perceive previously difficult forms and shapes as letters and words.

An important strength of the Winter Haven Program lies in the fact that it attempts to find out and remedy problems before the child has experienced repeated failure, and before the child's confidence in himself has been shattered. The children who are apt to have trouble learning are recognized and given perceptual training before they can become the traditional problem learners that exist in every classroom.

It would seem that Kephart and Lowder are echoing Comenius, Locke, Rousseau, and Pestalozzi in their emphasis on sensorimotor training. They begin in early childhood at the child's instructional level, proceed slowly from concrete to abstract, provide success, structure the environment, and attend to individual needs.

The philosophical and psychological foundations upon which

twentieth century educational theorists appear to have constructed their methods should be carefully considered by those concerned with organizing instruction for all children, not just those with a problem. The theory behind sensorimotor training should be of special interest to the educators of young children who have been called inefficient learners.

Chapter V

THE TEACHER OF INEFFICIENT LEARNERS

SINCE THE IMPORTANCE of the teacher in the educational process has become an accepted fact, it seems to follow that the teacher of inefficient learners should be carefully chosen and trained if we are to secure enough teachers and also the best teachers. Not only do we need the best teachers, but also teachers who are good for and good with the child who is having learning problems. Not all teachers have the necessary attributes. It is one thing to be a good teacher in an average middle-class public school classroom and quite another thing to be a good teacher in a public school classroom devoted to teaching children who are having problems learning.

Although there have been many surveys and studies made in an effort to determine just what it is that makes a good teacher, the only fact agreed upon is that no one can isolate any particular factor as the most important quality of good teachers. The problem of defining a good teacher of the inefficient learner is even more complicated.

This teacher must be all that any good teacher is, only more so! Children who have learned to distrust adults, and to work out problems by themselves are often placed in special classes which are inappropriate for their needs. This alone makes for a difficult job. Some teachers who are assigned to these classes are openly waiting for the day when they will have enough seniority to be transferred to a "better" class. These less desirable classes are usually assigned to the beginning teacher who is the least likely to be qualified for the job. What chance is there for the child who is not wanted anywhere, especially by his teacher?

PERCEPTION MUST BE EXCEPTIONAL

The teacher who is to help the inefficient learner must have a definite desire to do so. She must be in this position because she wants

The Teacher of Inefficient Learners 57

to be there. There must be something special in her makeup that differs from the ordinary. This person desires to do the difficult and succeed. There must be a good understanding of self and others, and confidence enough to accept a challenge. Above all else this teacher must be sensitive to her own needs and to the needs of others. She must be able to see things that others overlook. She must feel the needs of children even though they are unspoken. She must hear things that others do not hear when children talk. She must be equally good at hearing things children say when they do not talk. She must have an extra something that is undefinable and which cannot be given to her if she does not have it.

RAPPORT MUST BE ESTABLISHED

It is not an easy task to gain the trust of children who have learned to distrust adults. The teacher must be able to establish a satisfying relationship with the child since her effectiveness in motivating and reinforcing the child's learning will depend greatly upon this relationship. The child must know that he is accepted as he is. He must know that he is respected and appreciated as an individual. He must know that he is accepted and recognized regardless of his social status or academic status. The teacher must develop invisible antennae which are tuned in on the child's verbal and nonverbal messages. The messages are constantly being sent but not often received, translated, and acted upon.

The class must know that the teacher's main objective is not uniformity and standardization. This kind of teacher does not really like children nor does she understand them. She should not be in any classroom, but particularly not in one which requires the best teacher. Any teacher who considers her students inferior to herself because of social class, cultural background, intellectual capacity, or some other superficial standard is much too limited in her thinking to be of value to our special children. Any attempt to establish rapport would be spotted by the children as false. The teacher then becomes another "middle class do-gooder" who is as unreliable as tomorrow.

Our teacher must know that—clean or dirty, black, white, brown, or yellow, whole or crippled, from one side of town or the other, from the slums to the wealthy areas, her students are human beings, worthy of respect, each with valuable potentials which must be discovered and nurtured. If she honestly feels this, she will have little difficulty conveying the message to the children by her actions—not necessarily her mouth.

Beautiful buildings, planned by architects who have never taught, and abundant supplies are wasted if teachers are employed who cannot establish rapport with her pupils. On the other hand, if teachers are able to communicate properly with pupils, the physical plant becomes very unimportant.

COMPASSION MUST BE TEMPERED BY TOUGHNESS

The desire to discover and nurture children's potentials must be basic to the teacher but it must never become maudlin sympathy or an attitude of permissiveness. Compassion is present but it is controlled by enough toughness to enable the teacher to withstand the pressure. This teacher must be strong enough to see that rules are given—along with reasons for the rules, and she must remain in charge to see that the rules are carried out. The rules should be few and consistently enforced. Confrontations should be avoided when possible. The teacher should set a good example in politeness, honesty, and fairness.

It must be recognized that the teacher is responsible for her own classroom, and trips to the principal or some other higher authority are very rare. This fact must be recognized by teacher, student, principal, and parent. The teacher's efforts are useless if parental appeal to the principal will result in teacher rebuke.

REALISM HELPS

The successful teacher will have respect for high standards but will be realistic in her expectations. Unrealistic goals are often as defeating as no goals.

It is necessary to be realistic about giving of oneself. The teacher must be able to give without draining herself. It is not necessary to be consumed by doing one's job well. All teachers have a private life and so should our special teacher. She must be able to give freely and not artificially as the difference is easily detected. She must be willing to learn about the child, his environment, his special abilities and disabilities, and his motivation. What he will be interested in, what he will be motivated to do and what he can realistically be expected to do will be influenced by his surroundings.

The teacher who can learn about the child will have an advantage in helping him. It is not that we lower our standards—just that we are more realistic and adjust our expectations according to existing conditions. Rather than try to fit a child into an unrealistic curriculum, it would seem wiser to rearrange the curriculum to fit the child.

ACCEPTANCE AND FLEXIBILITY GO HAND IN HAND

The teacher must accept the children as they are and not be overanxious about their behavior. Their values and attitudes are often different from the teacher's and it is necessary to be flexible to adjust to the situation. The classroom may not always be quiet and in perfect order but that does not indicate that there is no learning taking place. If noise and motion are a way of life, then learning may take place in noise and motion. There must be order to the noise and motion but it is not wise to expect active children to sit and listen quietly for long periods of time. Small issues and small noises must be tuned out and not allowed to overwhelm the teacher. It is better to be concerned with larger issues and not be too concerned by that which cannot be changed.

By being flexible and adjusting to the situation as it exists, the teacher is often able to use the situation as a teaching technique. The study of rocks can be initiated as easily by a rock thrown through a window as by a rock purchased from a supply house.

If the needs of some of the students call for a reduction of stimuli, the teacher and students must realize the importance of making this provision for those who need it. Here is an opportunity to teach by example what is meant by respect for others.

CREATIVITY IS VITAL

Our very special teacher should be creative and innovative, yet tolerant of necessary restrictions and limitations. She must be willing to try new ideas and techniques and be able to create her own. Often some very useful manipulative device can be created by the teacher better than by someone not personally involved in the immediate situation. The teacher knows the ability of the learner, the desired learning, and the skill required. Materials and devices made by the teacher or by the learner himself are often more effective and always more personal. Many times the desired learning will take place during the creation of the device.

TEACHER TALKING SHOULD BE KEPT AT A MINIMUM

A task-oriented classroom is preferable to one in which the teacher tries to teach by talking and explaining. The tasks must be ones in which the learner has probability of success, yet they must allow for new and desired learnings to take place. This type of teaching requires flexibility on the part of the teacher as she must be concerned for groups and individuals and want to help them all learn how to learn. No longer can she make one lesson plan for the day which must be "corrected" by someone in the office. No longer can she make one lesson presentation for the entire class and then give an assignment which will be corrected and returned the next day or the next week—or never. The class will seldom be doing things as one group, rather several groups will be operating on several different topics, and several different levels, all at the same time. The teacher is organized enough to have well-planned tasks for the various groups, yet flexible enough to change when change is indicated.

This is not to imply chaos in the classroom. There is always teacher controlled structure and order is maintained, but with enough permissiveness to allow learning to take place for each individual—not just the one to whom the teacher happens to be talking at the moment.

DIPLOMACY IS REQUIRED

The teacher must be able to communicate equally well with students, their parents, other teachers, and the administration. If the communication is carried out diplomatically, all involved can be a useful resource to the teacher.

A SPECIAL HUMAN BEING IS NEEDED

The teacher must be reliable so that the child can count on her to do the expected. He has had enough of the unexpected. She must be dependable so that the child can count on her for emergencies, since he has been on his own long enough. She must be trustworthy so that the child can count on discretion, he has had little reason to trust adults. Often life has been a series of exhilarations and despair. He therefore needs a teacher who will structure his activities for him and provide some stability.

Emotional stability of the teacher is of utmost necessity. She must be consistent in all that she does and must not need the children to bolster her bent ego. Although this teacher must have a definite and sincere desire to help the child with a problem, this must never become an opportunity to unleash her unspent emotions. It is necessary to be able to control one's own emotions in any emergency. In this position, emergencies are frequent and varied. The teacher must be able to display acceptance without affection, and control without temper.

PREPARATION IS A WAY OF LIFE

All teachers need to know their teaching fields, but the teacher of the inefficient learner will need to know her teaching field and a variety of methods which will enable her to adapt material and create new techniques to suit the various needs of her children. There is little time to learn the needed techniques after the teacher steps into the classroom. There should be a good background of training and an understanding of basic techniques upon which the teacher can build day by day.

This is not to say that once a teacher has completed a preparatory course, has learned some of the techniques, and has begun to teach, that he is completely prepared for his teaching assignment. Preparation is never-ending, and learning should be never-ceasing. It is better to have five year's experience than one year's experience twenty times. Our very special teacher should be continually seeking newer and better techniques to accomplish realistic goals for the individuals for whom she has accepted responsibility.

TEACHER TRAINING

Not all individuals who seem desirous of working with inefficient learners are fitted to do so. There should be some facility for careful counseling and screening, if we are to achieve the goal of securing only those who will be best suited for this kind of work.

It is a useless waste to train the young, supremely dedicated student who is very sympathetic to the needs but who lacks empathy or stamina. Too often she becomes disillusioned after one year and is lost to the teaching profession permanently. More care needs to be given in choosing those to be trained. Some of this might conceivably take place at the high school level, and much more in the beginning stages of training.

Attention should be given to retraining experienced teachers who have demonstrated success in teaching. They have a background upon which to build and are often less apt to drop out. These must, however, be only those who have demonstrated success—not failure. It is a "sad state of affairs" when the teacher who has been a misfit in any job is given the more important job of teaching the special class because no one else will take it.

MONEY IS NOT THE ANSWER

Our teacher trainees must know that no amount of money and no financial endowment can change our disadvantaged learners into gifted learners. The change from inefficiency to efficiency must come about through the teachers and teachers of teachers.

Teacher training institutions must first realize that a government grant is not the answer to a problem. Too often the money is spent meeting the requirements of the proposal and not the needs of the future teachers. Likewise, they must realize that a good liberal arts program to give the middle-class teacher a good educational background is a far cry from her future needs as a teacher of the disadvantaged.

TEACHERS NEED TO STUDY CHILDREN

Too many teacher training programs operate as though they are completely unaware of the needs of teachers, particularly the needs of teachers of inefficient learners. It seems as though we have forgotten what it is we are to train for, and also what should be going on in the elementary and secondary school. Due to the explosion of knowledge, we have concentrated on providing the schools with subject matter specialists rather than child specialists. There may be much more information to be acquired by the student but up to now the baby is still being born with the same amount of information. Until a way is found to hasten growth and development, the information will still have to be acquired in sequence. We tend to believe or operate our schools as though we believe that all children in the United States are in the upper 2 percent of the population when it comes to learning subject matter.

It follows, then, that a minimum of education courses is desirable and all methods courses should be grouped into one or two large blocks. This serves to give the prospective teacher a brief ineffective overview of what education is all about.

It has become important for the prospective teacher to learn French or Spanish so that she can teach some of this to the grade school children whose language behavior she does not understand. It would seem to be more important for her to learn about children and how to teach them if this is what she is planning to do with her life. Many teachers are certified to teach who have been given no knowledge of differences in children and their individual needs.

Often there are special requirements above and beyond the four-year course, but these are so limited and evaluation so flexible that one or two extra courses will often certify a teacher of special education classes.

We know that the teacher of the inefficient learner should possess special skills, knowledges, and understandings. Since she was probably not born thus endowed, it seems we must find a way to provide for effective training.

It is of prime importance that the teacher be made to realize that she does not know all the answers, and dedication is not enough. She must want to learn and never cease learning. Her dedication may be accepted as long as it does not interfere with her teaching.

Close contact with inefficient learners should come early in the training program. Involvement should be with the whole family in community activities if possible. Student teaching should be done with the inefficient learners and it must be supervised by a superior teacher.

TEACHERS NEED TO LEARN HOW AND WHY

Methods courses should not be eliminated and combined as has now become rather a common practice. They are one of the most important courses for teachers of special children. No course can give the prospective teacher the answer as there is no answer—rather she will have the opportunity to learn many answers, some of which she may be able to put into practice. Since a large repertoire of methods and techniques is desirable, and since the prospective teacher must find some way to acquire this knowledge, it would seem that there is a need for many methods courses, modified to meet the needs of the individual learner.

PROGRAMS SHOULD BE PLANNED BY SUCCESSFUL TEACHERS

Teacher education needs more than a good public relations administrator to manage it. The tinkering with programs that is often done by an administrator who taught a year or two is often the most insurmountable obstacle to upgrading education. Too often the administrator of a special education program is most unfamiliar with teaching a special class.

If children often have difficulty reconciling home and school, and the middle-class teacher has difficulty reconciling her school with the community of children—how much more difficult for the administrator of the teacher-training program to reconcile his theory with practices! It is better to spend some time becoming involved in the community than to spend the junior year abroad. A knowledge of the lives and learning styles of children we expect to teach should provide a better background for establishing teacher-training programs.

The prospective teacher must have a growing knowledge of the literature in the field. She must not be satisfied with present knowledge and must continue to learn. This habit should be begun in the teacher-training program.

Teacher training must not confine itself to tools and methods, but must help teachers learn to ask the right questions more often than they give the right answers. It is necessary to learn just what knowledges are important for the learner. How much should he learn, and what should he learn? We must help our prospective teachers to realize that not all children need the same knowledges.

Courses in learning theory are important as well as courses in urban sociology and cultural anthropology. Availability of studies of the culture of poverty and characteristics and problems of minority groups should be of value to the prospective teacher. This teacher must be concerned with theory and research and must also be concerned with its practical application.

The liberal education for this teacher will be one that acquaints her with her teaching field, helps her to be a specialist in the teaching process, and helps her to know what education can do for people. Her preparation should not become a matter of accumulating credits in courses. The development of an attitude toward learning and discovery is vital to success.

Preparation must awaken to the fact that the traditional grade levels for which they are presently preparing teachers are of little meaning and the content taught is often inappropriate to the child with a learning problem.

Schools must train prospective teachers in the identification of inefficient learners. The teacher must not only recognize the fact that there is a problem, she must be skilled in identifying it. No school can have enough psychologists to examine every child who does not fit the teacher's preconceived mold. Not all students in the inner-city schools are disadvantaged. It is most important for the teacher to know which are and which are not. Developmental lags, sensory deprivation, and experiential deficits can and do occur in every type of home.

First-hand field experiences with inefficient learners are very important. They can help the teacher decide before she experiments on a room full of children whether or not she is "cut out" for this kind of work. It is better to decide before taking a job than to cause children to suffer the consequences of experimentation. There should be opportunities for observation, volunteer work, and participation whenever possible to familiarize the teacher with conditions under consideration. Listening to children and working with them will help to educate the prospective teacher to their needs, desires, and abilities.

There should also be a basic core of required courses in addition to the field experiences. The teacher must be cognizant of basic educational principles of learning and the learning process.

IN-SERVICE TRAINING

Quality in-service training should be part of teaching. This does not mean, necessarily, a series of faculty meetings presided over by an administrator who has a captive audience because teachers are required to attend. Neither does this mean a series of courses offered for credit which have been chosen by the administration, although both may be one effective method of in-service training.

The teacher's education really begins once she enters the classroom and it is to be hoped that it never ceases. Continuing education is as important as continuing preparation. Both are required of the professional educator.

To be sure that her classroom is not turned into a factory for pouring knowledge and skills into children, the teacher must be continually searching for means to make the classroom a workshop for learning. To teach children how to learn, how to seek more worthy goals, and to achieve more lasting satisfaction, the teacher must be learning, seeking more worthy goals, and trying to achieve more lasting satisfactions.

To keep abreast of new methods, expanded subject matter, and innovative textbooks is an immense job which must be accomplished. This task is made easier through in-service programs. Textbooks can be screened by competent members of the profession before being presented to the teachers' group. Conventions, meetings, and workshops could occupy more hours than there are in a day, but when one member visits or attends, in-service meetings can provide a valuable summary for all.

One good method of in-service training does not mean that there are not others—perhaps better. The teacher must continue to grow, expand knowledge, and be ready to accept any child brought to her.

Chapter VI

CLASSROOM MANAGEMENT

THERE CANNOT BE one plan dictated for a teacher to use in organizing her class as each class is composed of a variety of humans with different needs which must be met. The necessary basic structural procedures will of necessity be accommodated to the needs of the class and the personality of the teacher. This is not intended to excuse omission of any basic procedure but rather to allow for flexibility in execution.

The beginning teacher should have opportunity to study the accumulative folder of each child in her room prior to the beginning of the school year. There are other ways she can gather useful information and be better prepared to begin the year.

HOME VISITS

Although any teacher would be a better teacher if she could visit with the parents of her children, it is of vital importance to the teacher of children who are having problems learning.

One visit a year to the child's home is not enough and more should be encouraged. The first visit is the most important as it is the time when the teacher must establish rapport. In most instances a formal visit which has been prearranged is of very little value. An "accidental" informal meeting is usually more fruitful, but not always possible the first time. The first visit should take place before school starts and will therefore quite probably be prearranged. At this time the purpose is to let the parent know that the teacher wants to help the child. This impression must be deliberately given; it cannot be assumed. To many parents the school has become an enemy to be distrusted. It has proven to the parents that it cannot be trusted as it has failed their child. The child was not gifted enough to fit the school's plan or the teacher's academic program, and the parents have been made aware of this fact. It is time now for positive action.

They must be made to feel that some help is available and it is sincere. This one idea must be conveyed to the parents if their cooperation is to be secured.

The teacher will have little difficulty establishing the desired rapport if she forgets for a while that she has a college degree and is therefore a superior individual. She must be one person who cares about the child. She must not talk above or down to people. She is not there to give her learned advice. She is there to find out how she can help. Later parents may ask for advice and be ready to take it. While visiting, much useful information can be collected by observation—not direct questioning.

No matter what the condition of the home, the teacher must appear to be comfortable and at ease. If coffee is offered in a dirty cup, it must be accepted and enjoyed. In every home there is something in which to take pride. It may be a new baby, a handmade doily, a piece of furniture, or the television set, but whatever it is it must be noted. By noticing and complimenting, you can become a friend of the family.

If the first visit to the home has been a success, other visits during the year can be more satisfying and fruitful. Advice will be asked for and often will be taken, but it must be sought, not forced.

CHOOSE A SUITABLE BATTERY OF TOOLS FOR DIAGNOSIS

The information given in the accumulative folder of the child leaves much to be desired by the sincere teacher. It is helpful to choose a few diagnostic tools preparatory to planning remediation techniques. It would be most expedient if the teacher could have each child individually for a half day prior to the beginning of the school year. At this time she could use some instruments and some observation techniques to aid her in programming. Chapter VII will contain some suggested tools which may be used for this purpose.

PRESCRIBE A PROGRAM TO MEET INDIVIDUAL NEEDS

After seeing each child individually and using some instruments for diagnosis, a profile of weak areas should be apparent. This dictates the plan of action. It is necessary to set individual goals for each child and allow time in each school day for deliberate remediation of the weaknesses. The teacher then writes her objectives for each child and chooses some techniques for remediation. This will not consume the entire school day but will demand a separate period of time each day.

The school day is organized much as any class is organized. The day may begin with "show and tell," the National Anthem, the Pledge to the Flag, or any other group activity that is suitable. Whatever the beginning activity it must be consistently and rather rigidly adhered to as the child deserves this much security. He may come from a very disorganized situation or one of much insecurity and he deserves to know what he can expect when he gets to school.

Classes that must be scheduled depend upon the abilities of the individuals in the group. Because of the variety of abilities there must be several different levels of prereading or reading classes, many different levels of prenumber or arithmetic classes, as well as other academic subjects. While the teacher is working with one child or two or three children in one corner of the room on some subject or topic, the other children in the class must also be working independently or in small groups on some useful and purposeful activity. Hands that are busy are seldom in trouble. While the teacher is working with a few children in reading, the others may be working on Frostig worksheets, other worksheets that help ameliorate their weakness or even practicing on the balance beam in the far corner of the room. In this type of situation the children learn to respect others and social values need not be deliberately taught—they just happen.

The emotional and social needs of the children are met in this classroom in a natural way during every school day. They learn to respect the needs of others, they are given tasks to do at which they can succeed, and they are not made to feel inferior by anyone. They realize that they are receiving help by someone who cares, as is every other person in their class. They are not so different from their peers. Their emotional needs are also met through the establishment of a very definite and quite inflexible daily schedule of activities. They deserve the security of knowing in advance what to expect of school and what school expects of them.

SUGGESTED DAILY PROGRAM (VERY YOUNG CHILDREN)

Time	Activity	Description
9:00-9:15	Arrival	Established routines (coats, lunches, etc.).
9:15-9:30	Room chores	Collect lunch money, water plants, feed pets, rest room.
9:30-9:35	Opening exercises	
9:35-9:45	Snack time	Not only provides breakfast but gives opportunity for manners, language activities, sharing, waiting, and cleaning up.
9:45-10:00	Discussion	Language activities, news of the day, experience charts, etc.
10:00-10:30	Individualized activities for reading or reading readiness	Children work on individual materials. Teacher works with individual children. Definite routine, no-nonsense period.
10:30-11:00	Motor training	Children participate in group motor and perceptual training, not fun and games, free play, but work time.
11:00-11:30	Preparation for lunch	Need to wash, set table, fold napkins, rest room.
11:30-12:00	Lunch	A group activity to teach manners, good food habits. Children must clean up after lunch.
12:00-12:30	Rest time	Music may be played or just quiet time, rest room.
12:30-1:00	Story time	
1:00-1:30	Communication skills	Individual or group activities using multi-sensory approaches.
1:30-2:00	Arithmetic or pre-number activities	Individualized or group work on number readiness.
2:00-2:15	Preparation for dismissal	Established routines, rest room, reminders for following day.
2:15	Dismissal	

SUGGESTED DAILY PROGRAM
(INTERMEDIATE CHILDREN)

Time	Activity	Description
9:00-9:15	Opening exercises	Flag salute, National Anthem, etc.
9:15-9:45	Writing	Individual help
9:45-10:15	Arithmetic	Individual help
10:15-10:30	Rest room break	
10:30-11:30	Reading activities	(or perceptual training)
11:30-11:45	Preparation for lunch	
11:45-12:15	Lunch	
12:15-12:30	Rest time or quiet time	
12:30-1:00	Communication or language	
1:00-1:30	Social studies	
1:30-2:00	Motor training	
2:00-2:30	Arts and crafts for sense training	
2:30	Dismissal	

SUGGESTED DAILY PLAN (OLDER CHILDREN)

Time	Activity
8:30-9:30	Individual reading programs
9:30-10:00	Motor training—group or individual
10:00-11:00	Individual arithmetic
11:00-11:30	Perceptual training
11:30-12:00	Writing and spelling
12:00-12:30	Lunch
12:30-1:00	Story and question time
1:00-1:30	Social studies
1:30-2:00	Family living
2:00-2:30	Free time for activities or projects
2:30	Dismissal

SET REALISTIC GOALS

It is vital that realistic goals be set for child, parents, and teacher. We do not expect to make the retarded child gifted, nor should we expect similar miracles for the children with whom we are to work. We should, however, expect to see some progress.

Realistic goals must be given the parents not only in order that they will realize the advantage of encouragement but also the danger of pushing the child beyond his capabilities. This could only serve to compound his problems. The parent who can be helped to understand the problems will be in a better position to assist in the required remediation techniques. The parent must know what he can expect and what he cannot expect of the child and the school. Unrealistic hopes and dreams can lead only to more frustration and disappointment.

Realistic goals must be given the child as he is the one who must overcome his own problems with the help of the teacher. He must understand his problem and accept it as a temporary deterrent in order that he will cooperate in improvement techniques.

Realistic goals must be set for the teacher for her to function efficiently. She must not expect the impossible but must expect improvement. She must be continually evaluating to measure or determine whether or not her goals are being met. The goals must therefore be possible. If her goal for the child is that he be clean each day, she can easily achieve this goal by giving him a shower at school and providing him with nice clean clothes. If, however, her goal is for him to *want* to be neat and clean each day, she must not do this for him. He must accept the problem and the responsibility of doing these things for himself because he wants to do so. The teacher is not the mother, and her responsibility is to teach. She must then have some realistic idea of just how much she can expect to accomplish.

THE FIRST DAY

The first day of the school year is the most important one. This is the time when the children "size-up" the teacher, the teacher "sizes-up" the class, and faculty and staff "size-up" each other. It is the time of first impressions which must be accurate impressions for the class. This is the day when the discipline problems of the year are decided and solved. Not that rules are to be given and punishments set but that by her actions and behavior the teacher lets the class know that this is a no-nonsense classroom; humor is enjoyed but foolishness is banned. This she does by her behavior, words, and actions. The first day is well planned and busy. There is no time for foolishness and it is quickly dismissed.

Education is the main occupation of teacher and students and this idea is immediately conveyed by the atmosphere. We came to learn and this is how we will do it. Most of the first day's activities will be group activities, with a gradual subdivision into more and more small groups or individualization. By setting the stage for a learning environment many of the usual problems can be avoided.

The first day's activities must be those at which all of the children can feel success and little failure if any. Overplanning is better than underplanning, and no time is given to free play or unstructured activities.

DISCIPLINE

If the stage has been set correctly the first day, many discipline problems are avoided. This saves time and aggravation for teacher and student. The child has learned just how tolerant the teacher is and knows just what to expect. He deserves this security.

There are a few rules that can be given to a teacher who is concerned with discipline problems. These are really just good common sense, which many people believe does not exist. They have therefore given new terminology such as behavior modification to this common sense and made it quite an innovation.

Rules are made to be broken and so are these, but they are good guidelines.

1. Do not make rules—teach attitudes and concern for others.
2. Never threaten.
3. If you make a promise, keep it.
4. Never raise your voice.
5. Praise that which is desirable. Ignore that which is undesirable. Money, tokens, and candy are not necessary.
6. Never get excited. Unrewarded temper tantrums will subside.
7. If punishment is necessary, it must hurt. Spankings do not always hurt. Sometimes they are rewards in the eyes of the child.
8. Be strict and firm with understanding—not cruelty.

9. Be consistent and fair.
10. Let the child know you care and understand but do not tolerate misbehavior. You will help him correct it.

Although inner discipline is our goal for our children, they have a right to expect and receive outer discipline from us first until a gradual self-discipline can evolve.

INTEGRATION WITH OTHER CLASSES

In many school systems it has become the policy for the students in the special education classes to be integrated with the regular classes as much as possible. Physical integration seems to be synonymous with social and intellectual integration. This is a stretch of the imagination. Putting a child in with a group of normal children in a regular music, gym, or art class does not necessarily meet his needs. It could meet his needs if the regular teacher is also a special education teacher, understands his needs, and is able to provide for them. More often he is permitted to sit in the class and feel like a misfit because he is unable to successfully participate. This is a far cry from the definition of integration.

Not only does integration in other classes serve to show the child that he is different, but it cuts into the program of the special teacher so that she does not have ample time to work with the child on his individual problem. The child who needs special help because of temper tantrums does not often arrange his tantrums to fit the schedule of other teachers. He needs to be with his own teacher when the tantrums occur so that she will be in a position to handle the problem. Other problems are equally inconsiderate of the daily program of the school.

The child is entitled to the consistency of one teacher all day at least in the beginning stages of remediation. He has enough problems to overcome without having to learn different schedules, different teachers' personalities, and different routes to classes.

It is hoped that the time will come when the child has overcome enough of his problems so that he can be integrated in other classes successfully. That is, he can be a part of the learning situation and not apart from it.

PUBLIC RELATIONS

The special teacher must be a firm believer in what she is doing and she must know how to convey this to others on the staff. Some staff members take offense to the word *special* because they are ignorant of the situation. They have probably seen special teachers who are not worthy of the name, and there are many of these. The special teacher who appears to have much free time when her children are dismissed early is deserving of the criticism she will receive. This should be a work period.

It is important to be a part of the school system and convey this attitude to fellow staff members. Sharing of ideas and materials can be mutually beneficial. Although it is often quite difficult to communicate with administrators who have had absolutely no background in special education, it is vital to the success of the program that they be cooperative.

The teacher, not the social worker or school nurse, should be the public relations person who contacts parents. She is the one who knows the situation and should also be the one who relates this to parents. She must believe in what she is doing and be able to sell the idea to others.

Chapter VII

DIAGNOSTIC TOOLS AND PRESCRIPTIVE PLANNING

THE POOR TEACHING practices that have been given as one of the causes for children's learning problems are not limited to the regular classroom. Many special education teachers are equally guilty. Sorting children and assigning them to a particular classroom with a teacher who has "taken" certain prescribed courses is not necessarily the answer to the problem. It may very well be the solution to the problem if the teacher is able to determine what problems the child is having and initiate some form of remediation or therapy.

After the child has been found eligible for special class placement, the special teacher usually will receive his accumulative folder and the psychological report. The report of the school nurse is usually included. This will provide a brief overview of the home and family. Usually the occupation of the parents, number of siblings, condition of the house, and subjective comments of the interviewer will be given.

The report from the psychologist will contain information about the child's personality and any emotional problems, with much conjecture regarding the cause. This is of particular value to the teacher of emotionally disturbed children, who have deliberately not been discussed in this text. However, this information could also be of value to the teacher of inefficient learners as there may be emotional problems present which have been caused by the learning problem. Should this be the situation, the psychologist usually provides needed advice and direction. The reader who works with emotionally disturbed children is referred to some of the numerous texts concerned with that problem.

Seldom is the psychological report of much practical value to the teacher who must plan the program for children who are having

Diagnostic Tools and Prescriptive Planning 77

learning problems. She must become skilled in locating the problem or problems herself. The first information that is given her is the psychologist's report, which has much useful information if she knows how to find it.

The confidential report of the psychologist is just that—confidential. The information in it should be kept to those who are working with the child. Too often the special teacher is given the report after the secretaries and other personnel have finished reading it. This report usually contains results of an individually administered intelligence test. Although this is usually interpreted to the teacher as a measure of intelligence, the subtest results may also be used as a diagnostic tool for programming individual remediation. Although a few school psychologists still use the Binet, many have learned the value of the Wechsler Intelligence Scale for Children (WISC). This is not a test for teachers to use, as it must be administered by a qualified psychologist. Knowledge of the results of the subtests should be given to the teacher, and she should know the meaning of each subtest.

WECHSLER INTELLIGENCE SCALE FOR CHILDREN

This test is divided into two sections, verbal and performance. These are the subtest areas.

A. Verbal Tests
   1. General Information
      a. Gained from experience and education
      b. Alertness to world around him
      c. Social awareness
      d. Associative thinking
   2. General Comprehension
      a. Common sense
      b. Social judgment
      c. Cultural background
      d. Practical knowledge
      e. Reasoning
   3. Arithmetic
      a. Mental alertness
      b. Arithmetic reasoning
      c. Concentration of attention

    d. Visualization
    e. Auditory memory
  4. Similarities
    a. Logical thinking
    b. Abstract thinking
    c. Concepts
  5. Vocabulary
    a. Word knowledge gained from experience and schooling
    b. Fund of information
  6. Digit Span
    a. Attention and concentration
    b. Memory
    c. Auditory perception
B. Performance Tests
  1. Picture Completion
    a. Visual alertness
    b. Visual memory
    c. Recognition of details
    d. Conceptual abilities
    e. Perceptual abilities
  2. Picture Arrangement
    a. Interpretation and social situation
    b. Social intelligence
    c. Attention to details
  3. Block Design
    a. Ability to perceive pattern
    b. Ability to analyze whole parts
    c. Ability to synthesize the parts to form abstract design
    d. Visual motor coordination
    e. Abstract thinking
    f. Ability to plan and organize
  4. Object Assembly
    a. Putting together simple puzzles
    b. Perception of the whole and relation of the parts
    c. Visual motor coordination
    d. Spatial relationships
  5. Coding
    a. Visual perception

Diagnostic Tools and Prescriptive Planning

    b. Speed of learning and writing symbols
    c. Manual dexterity
 6. Mazes
    a. Ability to work mazes
    b. Eye-hand coordination

The Wechsler Preschool and Primary Scale of Intelligence may be used. This is for children from four to six and one-half years of age. It is composed of eleven subtests grouped into two categories, verbal and performance. Eight of the subtests were scaled down from the WISC and three new ones were added.

A. Verbal
  1. General Information
  2. Vocabulary
  3. Arithmetic
  4. Similarities
  5. Sentences (new)
    a. Auditory memory
    b. Auditory perception
B. Performance
  1. Animal House (new)
    a. Similar to coding
  2. Picture Completion
  3. Mazes
  4. Geometric Design
    a. Visual perception
    b. Eye-hand coordination
  5. Block Design

By using the subtest scores, the teacher will be able to note weak areas which need remediation. The suggested techniques that are listed here will be only the beginning for a creative teacher. There can be no cookbook recipes given which will work with every child. Although some of the techniques suggested may work equally well in different areas, this is harmonious with a plan for a multisensory approach to remediation.

SUGGESTED REMEDIAL TECHNIQUES

Verbal, General Information

 1. Pictures and stories of holidays.

2. Monthly calendar.
3. Have the children make occasional cards for each other or for their parents.
4. Map games.
5. Opaque projector—draw silhouettes and map outlines.
6. Have the children write an autobiography with words or pictures.
7. Write individual or group biographies of famous people.
8. Weekly Reader or newspaper.
9. Awareness of seasons and months and their order.
10. Make a sentence about a picture.
11. Experience charts.
12. Field trips.
13. Puppets—write stories of history or current events and act them out through puppets.
14. Films and filmstrips.
15. Scrapbooks of occupations.
16. Discuss pictures and have children repeat stories.
17. "Let's pretend" games (you are George Washington).

Verbal, General Comprehension

1. Use pictures showing similar functions and describe why.
2. Games of association.
3. Draw geometric forms with dots and ask how the forms can be made larger, smaller.
4. Discuss pictures showing cause and effect (wrecked car—how did it get that way).
5. "What will happen if" games (. . . I stick a balloon with a pin?).
6. Situation games (There is a fire—what do you do? At first give the child two decisions and have him tell why he chose one).
7. Write a sentence that describes or goes with a picture.
8. Matching pictures.
9. Put what is missing in a picture.
10. Make a scrapbook of good manners.
11. Sort pictures as to funny, sad, etc.
12. Imitating games (Show me how to look tired, happy, etc.).

13. Role playing—act out social situations.
14. Write different types of leters.
15. Charades—expressing feelings.
16. Discuss stories as to the way the characters feel and act and explain why.
17. Children make up stories about what they would like to be when they grow up.
18. Make a story or scrapbook of "somebody I like or admire."
19. Collect and discuss news events.
20. Write or tell a story about community workers.
21. Have the children help plan and organize field trips.
22. Discuss behavior and rules and the reasons for them.
23. Play games—taking turns.
24. Make posters showing safety rules.
25. Have a social club.
26. Plays—sociodrama.
27. Puppet shows.
28. Plan and lay out a town, farm, etc., with all the community jobs.
29. Make diagrams of good behavior or considerate acts.
30. Discuss qualities of a good friend, brother, etc.
31. Have a child act as a big brother to a new child.
32. Play house, store, etc.
33. Give children specific room responsibilities.
34. Act out the use of an object.

Verbal, Arithmetic

1. Clap, tap, jump as you count.
2. Hop scotch—count orally.
3. Help with lunch count and attendance.
4. Simon Says—include: up, down, over, under, middle, front, etc.
5. Tens and ones—make ones-squares, tens-circles; make ones-red, tens-green.
6. Commercial games such as Fish.
7. Number lines; flash cards.
8. Throw bean bags in holes in cardboard—each hole has own value.

9. Tap out number combination—child taps out answer.
10. Twister.
11. Listening games and records.
12. Tape recorder.
13. Locate the sound.
14. Describe a sound—loud, soft, fast, slow.
15. Toy telephone.
16. Story sounds.
17. Cookie jar (from TC series).
    Rhythmically in unison:
    Group: Who stole the cookie from the cookie jar?
              Jane stole the cookie from the cookie jar.
    Jane: Who, me?
    Group: Yes, you.
    Jane: Couldn't be.
    Group: Then who?
    Jane: Billy stole the cookie from the cookie jar.
    Billy: Who, me?
           Etc.
18. Repeat nonsense rhymes.
19. Grandmother's Trunk.
20. Follow oral direction.
21. Play restaurant—waiter takes order; cook delivers; customers must pay if they get what they ordered.
22. Wrong word—teacher says three words; one does not fit.
23. Arrange objects on a table—teacher describes one and child must figure out which object it is.
24. Read a story and write a series of True-False questions.
25. Mother May I.
26. Tin can telephone.
27. Giants and Dwarfs: Leader says, "giants" and all must stand on their tiptoes; leader says, "men" and all stand naturally; leader says, "dwarfs" and all stoop down.
28. Bring me: Call child's name and say, "Bring me . . ." **If it is movable, he must bring it to you (pencil). If it is not movable, the child must stand still (window).**
29. You Must—played in the same manner as Simon Says.

30. Repeat a series of numbers—backward and forward.
31. Repeat simple letters and words.

Verbal, Similarities

1. How are things alike? (apples, pears, etc.)
2. Sort anything (colors, shapes, etc.).
3. Classify—pictures.
4. Scrapbooks (similar objects grouped in each section).
5. Show two pictures: What is different? What is alike?
6. Compare pictures for function and use.
7. Make two shapes. Cut one in pieces and have child assemble cut shape on the original shape.
8. Continental press materials.
9. Teacher-made materials (color all the squares; color all the fruits).
10. Place several objects on a table; tell how the things go together.
11. Use a picture of a zoo; cut out and paste all animals that live in a zoo (this can be done with anything—city, farm, school, etc.).
12. Match boxes and lids (jars and covers; pegs and holes.).
13. Place three similar and one different shape on a table; child picks out the one that is different. Repeat blindfolded.
14. Tactile Bag (feel inside to "see" what is in it).
15. Sort buttons according to size, shape, color, etc.
16. Stick-O-Mats and Color Shapes by Judy.
17. Taste Box—sort according to sweet/sour.
18. Smell Box—sort according to fragrant/sweet/pungent/putrid.
19. Old Maid.
20. Picture Rummy.
21. Match milk cartons filled with rice, stones, marbles, etc. (need two of each).
22. Tree leaves—how they are alike and/or different.

Verbal, Vocabulary

1. Bingo: cards can be made to deal with new words, antonyms, synonyms.

2. Scrapbooks—list words, sentences, or paragraphs dealing with each picture.
3. Word games: Say the opposite (antonym) of _____. What sounds like _____?
4. Have the child list all action words after listening to or reading a story.
5. Use toy phones—have children discuss a topic.
6. Child has a copy of a story (even his own) and substitutes synonyms for as many words as possible.
7. Have child tell about various pictures.
8. Group story—each child contributes a sentence.
9. Have child make up riddles (Example: I have a long neck and spots on my back. What am I?).
10. After hearing or reading a story, a child makes a "moving-picture box" in which he draws pictures on a roll of paper, puts in box, and retells story.
11. Child tells ending of a story the teacher starts.
12. Child simply defines words teacher gives him.
13. Word dominoes.
14. Picture dictionary.
15. Commercial games—Lotto, Scrabble.
16. Ask "what-why" questions.
17. Name all the objects found in a particular place or related to a particular use.
18. Child names objects in pictures.
19. Give a definition to child; he must pick the correct word from a group.

Verbal, Digit Span

1. Child, with his back turned or his eyes blindfolded, identifies different sounds (pencils being sharpened, tearing paper, etc.).
2. Child lists as many sounds as he can hear at a certain time (natural, background sounds).
3. Ring a bell in different parts of the room and have the blindfolded child point to the sound.
4. Use tape recorders, records, musical and rhythm instruments.

5. Read aloud jingles; have child tell which words rhyme.
6. Have child listen to record and pick out a certain melody or instrument sound.
7. Teach child simple songs—sing a line and have child repeat.
8. Simon Says.
9. Child repeats a sentence using same inflection the teacher did.
10. Child follows verbal direction: close the window, stand up.
11. Child repeats teacher's stamping, finger snapping, or clapping; sometimes blindfold the child.
12. Have the child repeat numbers in sequence and then backwards.
13. Read a simple paragraph to a child and ask him questions about it.
14. Each child has picture or toy of animal and brings it to the teacher when she makes that animal sound.
15. One child leaves the room; the rest of the children are sitting in a circle. One hides a small bell in his hand. Child returns and all children shake their hands in the air, and he guesses who has the bell.
16. Names and rhythm—teacher says child's full name and beats its rhythm with a drum. Later, child responds to just the drum rhythm.
17. Give a series of words that rhyme, with one word that does not rhyme. Have a child tell which word does not rhyme.
18. Tap on desk, glass, paper, blackboard, and on other objects in the room while children are looking the other way. They should try to name the object tapped.
19. Blindfold one child and ask one of the others to call out his name. The blindfolded child tries to identify child who called him.
20. Teach children jingles and nursery rhymes.
21. Tell the children a short story and have them repeat it as closely as possible to the original; increase its length.
22. Tap on desk or clap and ask children how many times you have tapped or clapped. Start with few taps, increasing the number.

Performance, Picture Completion

1. Make use of commercially prepared materials from Continental Press.
2. Show child a completed line drawing. Present same drawing with missing parts and let child draw the missing parts.
3. Show child a picture of a familiar animal. Tell him one part of the animal is missing. Show him pictures of animal parts. Ask him to identify missing part.
4. Give the child a plain colored cardboard that has a geometric shape cut from the middle. Give him several shapes. Ask him to point out the one that will fit, then put it in place.
5. Outline a face. Give child pictures of parts of face. Ask him to put them in the correct place.
6. Use jigsaw puzzles that stress pieces to form wholes.
7. Play games such as "What does not belong in this picture or group of words?"
8. Use phonics—blend wheel.
9. Complete geometric forms.
10. Ask child to identify letters omitted from a word.
11. Play charades.

Performance, Picture Arrangement

1. Use commercially prepared materials, such as See-Quees.
2. Give three or more pictures to child, after telling him a story; ask him to arrange them in proper sequence.
3. Teacher may tell story to group of children. Ask each child to draw one part of the story. The group may then arrange pictures in logical order.
4. Ask child to draw a picture by following dots, numerals, or letters.
5. Divide a large square into nine small squares. Number each square at random. Ask the child to jump from squares 1 through 9 in sequence.
6. Use story cut-ups. Teacher may read a story to the class, which is within their reading vocabulary or level of reading. Teacher then may cut the story into sentences. Give

Diagnostic Tools and Prescriptive Planning

one sentence to each child. Ask the children who has the first sentence, who has the second, etc.
7. Give child sentences in which words have been scrambled. Ask him to put words in proper order.
8. Ask child to make sentences from an assortment of words.
9. Make sentences from phrases.
10. Read a familiar rhyme, omitting some words. Ask children to supply the missing words.
11. Give a number sequence which is out of order. Let the child correct it.
12. Say to child, "Pretend you are going outside to play." Show him pictures of outdoor clothing. Ask him to indicate order in which he will dress himself.

Performance, Block Design

1. Copying figures.
2. Putting together models.
3. Puzzles.
4. Stencils to teach shapes.
5. Copying designs.
6. Making your own jigsaw puzzles.
7. Make miniature town, farms, or zoos (take these apart and discuss why they are grouped together).
8. Reproduce designs on paper or peg board with colored beads or colored blocks.
9. Chinese checkers.
10. Checkers.
11. Mosaics.
12. Parquetry.
13. Craftwork with tiles.
14. Cut out a picture of an object (a car, a house, etc.), cut in separate pieces, and have the child reassemble.

Performance, Object Assembly

1. Puzzles.
2. Identify an object from seeing just part of the picture—adding the missing parts.
3. Outline forms, animals, or people.

4. Follow outline in clay with fingertips.
5. Walk and crawl around shapes (a square or a circle, etc.).
6. Try to reproduce a picture or an object when given parts (snowmen, house, etc.) using pegboard and round head beads.
7. Dress paper dolls.
8. Put together models.
9. Match lids and different size jars.
10. Look at a picture from one angle; show the same picture at a different view or angle and have child identify object from different views or angles.
11. Scribble drawings.
12. Start a story for the child and let him finish it.

Performance, Coding

1. Copy forms from memory.
2. What's missing game.
    a. Objects on table—remove one.
    b. Words on board—erase one.
    c. Who left the room?
3. Concentration.
4. Show a picture, remove it, ask questions about it.
5. Show a pattern, remove it, child duplicates it.
6. Child in front of room; leaves; class describes his physical appearance.
7. Put objects into box; child views briefly; child describes what he saw.
8. Touch game: First person touches and names object; second person does same but adds another object.
9. Domino matching: Show one, remove it, and ask child to pick one that matches.
10. Direction ball: Children seated in circle; follow commands of "pass ball left," "pass ball right," etc.; may use music.
11. Singing games: Looby Loo, Hokey Pokey.
12. Simon Says.
13. On paper, color objects by following teacher's oral direction regarding directionality.
14. Match handprints.

Diagnostic Tools and Prescriptive Planning 89

15. Ditto handprints and footprints and give directions—Put ring on left little finger, string on right thumb, etc.
16. Have child place cardboard cutouts over corresponding shapes and sizes.
17. Draw or mark on left corner, right corner of paper according to directions. See also Nos. 1-30 in "Mazes."

Performance, Mazes

1. Paddle ball.
2. Jacks.
3. Marbles.
4. Tip it.
5. Bean bags.
   a. Catch it in bottle.
   b. Pitch at returning net.
6. Handball—variations.
7. Tracing simple pictures.
8. Follow the dots.
9. Cutting and pasting.
10. Ring toss.
11. Drop clothespins in a bottle.
12. Stencils and templates.
13. Color dittoed outlines.
14. Stringing beads.
15. Three-dimensional block building.
16. Jigsaw puzzles.
17. Pegboards.
18. Copy designs on paper.
19. Sewing cards.
20. Clock game (Kephart).
21. Toss objects in time to music.
22. Screw lids on jars.
23. Hand puppets.
24. Pinch clothespin on and off box.
25. Poke soap bubbles and balloons.
26. Cut clay with knife or scissors.
27. Practice on bolt board.
28. Practice button, zip, and tie.

29. Typing.
30. Erector set and tinker toys.
31. Tearing paper.
32. Sorting.
33. Make scrapbooks.
34. Grouping similar objects.
35. Unscramble disordered pictures.
36. Move through maze according to directions.

This is a beginning for the teacher who desires to help the inefficient learner. Much more information is needed. The observation and perception of the teacher is the determining factor, but there are several tools that may be used for evaluation of the child's disabilities and abilities. Some of these which may be used by the researcher will be listed. It must be remembered that this is only a sample of the available instruments, and others may be chosen or devised by the diagnostic teacher. It is wise to be cautious about believing that the cause of the problem has been found if one instrument provides some answers. Seldom does the child have only one problem. Even if he had only one problem in the beginning, he has probably acquired several by the time he gets to the special teacher.

One of the first areas of concern to the teacher is the physical condition of the child. Although most schools require a medical examination by a physician periodically, this seldom supplies the needed information. This report usually contains information concerning any serious illness, obvious deformity, immunization, condition of the teeth, and other useful information that the parent has given the doctor. In addition, the school nurse usually gives the standard vision screening test on the wall which will tell us if the child has vision problems. Any child who is having a problem learning is entitled to the five minutes required to administer a more accurate screening test.

VISUAL ACUITY
The Keystone Telebinocular

The Telebinocular is distributed by the Keystone View Company, Meadville, Pennsylvania. It can be used by the school nurse, the teacher, or anyone who has had the small amount of training required. This instrument provides a good survey of the visual equipment of the child. The materials are mounted on cards and placed in the Telebinocular, much like a stereoscope. This test is very comprehensive and evaluates the coordination of the eyes. It is preferred to reading from the wall chart twenty feet distant.

The Telebinocular can be used to evaluate visual acuity in these areas:

1. Simultaneous vision at far points.
2. Vertical posture, muscle balance.
3. Lateral postural balance at far point.
4. Fusion at far point, the eyes focusing and staying together.
5. Usable vision, both eyes far point, test of eye fatigue.
6. Usable vision, right eye.
7. Usable vision, left eye.
8. Stereopsis, depth perception.
9. Color vision.
10. Lateral posture (balance) at near point.
11. Fusion at near point.
12. Usable vision at near point, right eye.
13. Usable vision at near point, left eye.
14. Usable vision at near point, both eyes.

If the child fails this test, he should be referred to a specialist for further examination. He might also need training designed to strengthen the weaknesses.

For specific training techniques in visual perception, the reader is referred to *The Physiology of Readiness*, by G. N. Getman and Dr. Elmer R. Kane. This book provides six detailed programs which are extremely explicit and readable.

Program 1: Practice in Bilateral Action (Alternating Actions and Exploration of Body Parts)

The purpose of the practice is to have children explore and develop their body parts and the coordination of head, arms, body, and legs to gain greater freedom of skill of movement. Practice in general coordination provides the specific experiences and goal-directed action in total body movement that most children miss. These activities can be woven into classroom activities, playground period, or carefully elaborated in the gym during physical education class.

Program 2: Practice in Balance (Walking Beam Activities)

The purpose is to have children explore and develop the interrelationships of the sides of their bodies, movements involved in balance, and to have these movements visually directed. The key concept involved is the development of visual steering.

Program 3: Practice in Eye-Hand Coordination (Chalkboard Routines)

The purpose is to give children the opportunity to learn that hands work together as a pair, to give children opportunities to use eyes and hands as a team for the perceptions required in school work, and to coordinate the visual-tactual systems as a foundation for symbolic interpretations. When better coordination of the body parts is achieved and is led by visual steering, both attention span and span or recognition of symbols is improved.

Program 4: Practice in Eye Movements (Finger Jumps and Eye Pursuit Movements)

The purpose is to develop the control and accuracy of eye movements required in learning tasks, to learn ocular fixations to inspect symbols and forms, to learn ocular span so the child can select the important item from among many, to learn ocular sweep to enable the child to read a line of symbols such as a line of print. The preschool years do not provide much more than general and random patterning of eye movements, while the classroom uses a more specialized and directionally oriented type of eye movement for which the child is generally unprepared and which schools do not generally teach systematically.

Program 5: Practice in Form Perception (Chalkboard Templates and Desk Templates)

The purpose is to assist children to develop abilities to visually perceive forms as a) a prerequisite to symbol interpretation, b) integration of eye-hand actions for visual-tactual information, c) to develop perceptions of size, shape, likenesses, etc., basic to symbolic interpretations, d) to develop the comprehension of basic forms, and e) to develop kinesthesis (muscle feel) of the directions of movement.

Children's perceptions of forms and symbols depend more upon the motor act of making or drawing a form than upon the act of visual inspection. The use of the templates provides children with a motor-visual combination which is essential to symbolic recognition and interpretation.

Program 6: Practice in Visual Memory (Basic Forms, Double Forms, Open or Incomplete Forms, etc.)

The purpose is to help children explore and develop skills in recall and in accurate visualizations of previous experiences. The ability to recall a previous experience gives the child a frame of reference for new experiences and he can more accurately make discrimination of the new problem facing him.

AUDITORY ACUITY

It is essential that some test of auditory acuity be given by a qualified person. Most schools have sufficient funds to provide an audiometer and someone to use it correctly. This is the most accurate and reliable means to test the hearing of a child.

Wepman Auditory Discrimination Test

This short test takes very little time to administer but gives a picture of problems in auditory discrimination. This is obtained from J. M. Wepman, 950 East 59th Street, Chicago, Illinois 60637. This test can be administered by anyone who has a little practice using it. Twenty pairs of words are pronounced, and the child has only to determine if they sound the same or different. This test should give a picture of the child's ability to discriminate between sounds.

Marianne Frostig Developmental Test of Visual Perception

This test is available from Consulting Psychologists Press in Palo Alto, California. It is to be administered by the teacher and can be used individually or in small groups. The test has five sections.
1. Eye-motor coordination. The child is required to draw continuous straight, curved, or angled lines between boundaries without guide lines.
2. Figure-ground. The child is required to perceive pictures and figures hidden in increasingly complex backgrounds.

3. Constancy of shape. The child must recognize certain geometric shapes presented in a variety of sizes and positions.
4. Position in space. The child must be able to discriminate figures which are reversed or rotated in the series.
5. Spatial relationships. The child is required to copy lines of various lengths and angles, using dots and guidelines.

If a weak area is found, there are numerous workbooks and worksheets designed by Frostig to ameliorate the problem.

MOTOR EFFICIENCY

Of the many techniques available for assessing motor efficiency, three were chosen as basic to diagnosing specific difficulties in sensorimotor functioning. These were designed for teachers of children who have learning problems.

Psychoeducational Inventory of Basic Learning Abilities

This evaluation was designed by Robert Valett and is available from Fearon Publishers in Palo Alto, California. This is an individual evaluation and is not a standardized test. The observation of the examiner is quite important, as it is in other scales.

Educational tasks that are assessed are grouped into six major areas of learning. There are three levels of tasks, level B for ages 5-8, level M for ages 8-10, and level A for ages 10-12. Fifty-three basic learning abilities are to be evaluated.

A. Gross Motor Development
 1. Rolling
 2. Sitting
 3. Crawling
 4. Walking
 5. Running
 6. Throwing
 7. Jumping
 8. Skipping
 9. Dancing
 10. Self-identification
 11. Body localization
 12. Body abstraction
 13. Muscular strength

Diagnostic Tools and Prescriptive Planning

    14. General physical health
B. Sensorimotor Integration
    15. Balance and rhythm
    16. Body-spatial organization
    17. Reaction-speed dexterity
    18. Tactile discrimination
    19. Directionality
    20. Laterality
    21. Time orientation
C. Perceptual-Motor Skills
    22. Auditory acuity
    23. Auditory decoding
    24. Auditory-vocal association
    25. Auditory memory
    26. Auditory sequencing
    27. Visual acuity
    28. Visual coordination and pursuit
    29. Visual-form discrimination
    30. Visual figure-ground differentiation
    31. Visual memory
    32. Visual-motor memory
    33. Visual-motor fine muscle coordination
    34. Visual-motor spatial-form manipulation
    35. Visual-motor speed of learning
    36. Visual-motor integration
D. Language Development
    37. Vocabulary
    38. Fluency and encoding
    39. Articulation
    40. Word attack skills
    41. Reading comprehension
    42. Writing
    43. Spelling
E. Conceptual Skills
    44. Number concepts
    45. Arithmetic processes
    46. Arithmetic reasoning
    47. General information

48. Classification
49. Comprehension
F. Social Skills
50. Social acceptance
51. Anticipatory response
52. Value judgments
53. Social maturity

A profile chart is provided in order that a picture of weak areas will be given. The author of the inventory has also provided for remediation techniques in his handbook, *The Remediation of Learning Disabilities,* available from Fearon Publishers. This useful handbook is organized in such a manner that the teacher need only turn to the section devoted to any one of the fifty-three tasks assessed to find many ideas for initiating remediation.

Purdue Perceptual-Motor Survey

The Purdue Perceptual-Motor Survey was designed by Eugene G. Roach and Newell C. Kephart for the teacher to use as a tool to identify perceptual-motor difficulties in the child who is having learning problems. The survey is available from Charles E. Merrill Books, Inc., as is *The Slow Learner in the Classroom* by Dr. Kephart. This text should be studied by the teacher for two reasons. Firstly, it provides a basic understanding of theory underlying the scale, and secondly, it contains a section of training exercises which were designed to match the survey.

The survey is composed of twenty-two scorable items which are subdivided into eleven sections. Each is designed to measure some area of perceptual-motor development. The directions that are given for administering and scoring the survey are most detailed and explicit. A record form and a summary sheet are provided for a profile of each child. The items are grouped into five observable areas.

A. Balance and Postual Flexibility
  1. Walking board
  2. Jumping
B. Body Image and Differentiation
  1. Identification of body parts
  2. Imitation of movement
  3. Obstacle course

       4. Kraus-Weber
       5. Angels-In-The-Snow
   C. Perceptual-Motor Match
       1. Chalkboard
       2. Rhythmic writing
   D. Ocular Control
       1. Ocular pursuits
   E. Form Perception
       1. Visual achievement forms

Even though the child may have no obvious motor problems and appears to be quite normal in his development, weak areas can be identified by the use of the survey. The reader who doubts this has only to administer this survey to any primary grade class and match the profiles with the child's academic achievement to witness the similarities.

The Lincoln-Oseretsky Motor Development Scale

This scale by William Sloane, published by C. H. Stoelting Company, Chicago, was adapted from the Oseretsky Tests of Motor Proficiency. This test is primarily one of motor proficiency for children between the ages of six and fourteen.

Although the manual reminds us that this scale is still in experimental form and suggests needed research, the tasks do appear to sample a wide range of motor abilities. This is an individually administered scale which consists of thirty-six items. The manual contains explicit directions for administration and scoring. For the teacher who must diagnose and prescribe for children who are above the age range of the Purdue Perceptual-Motor Survey, the Lincoln-Oseretsky Motor Development Scale could be a useful tool.

The tasks are presented in order of difficulty.
   1. Walking backwards
   2. Crouching on tiptoe
   3. Standing on one foot
   4. Touching nose
   5. Touching fingertips
   6. Tapping rhythmically with feet and fingers
   7. Jumping over a rope
   8. Finger movement

9. Standing heel to toe
10. Closing and opening the hands alternately
11. Making dots
12. Catching a ball
13. Making a ball
14. Winding thread
15. Balancing a rod crosswise on the index finger
16. Describing circles in the air
17. Tapping
18. Coins and matchsticks
19. Jumping in the air making an about face, landing on tiptoes, and holding balance for three seconds
20. Putting matchsticks in a box
21. Winding thread while walking
22. Throwing a ball
23. Sorting matchsticks
24. Drawing lines
25. Cutting a circle
26. Putting coins in a box
27. Tracing mazes
28. Balancing on tiptoe
29. Tapping with feet and fingers
30. Jumping and touching heels
31. Tapping feet and describing circles with fingers
32. Standing on one foot with eyes closed
33. Jumping and clapping
34. Balancing on tiptoe
35. Opening and closing hands
36. Balancing a rod vertically

As the manual presents no remediation techniques, the teacher who detects weak areas in this scale must devise means to strengthen the child's motor functioning.

The Illinois Test of Psycholinguistic Abilities

In its experimental form this test (ITPA) consisted of nine subtests. This has been revised and now includes twelve subtests grouped according to levels and processes.

I. Representational Level

Diagnostic Tools and Prescriptive Planning

- A. Receptive Processes (Decoding)
    1. Auditory reception—the ability to understand what is heard
    2. Visual reception—the ability to understand what is seen
- B. The Organizing Process (Association)
    1. Auditory-vocal association—the ability to draw relationships from what is heard
    2. Visual-motor association—the ability to draw relationships from what is seen
- C. The Expressive Process (Encoding)
    1. Verbal expressive (vocal encoding)—the ability to express ideas verbally
    2. Manual expressive (motor encoding)—the ability to express ideas through gestures

II. Automatic Level
- A. Closure (Ability to integrate units into a whole)
    1. Grammatical closure—ability to respond automatically to common verbal expressions
    2. Auditory closure—ability to produce complete word from an incomplete one through organization of the parts
    3. Sound blending—ability to synthesize separate parts of words and produce the whole
    4. Visual closure—ability to identify a common object from an incomplete visual presentation
- B. Sequential Memory
    1. Auditory sequential memory—ability to reproduce from memory a series of symbols presented auditorily
    2. Visual-sequential memory—ability to reproduce sequences of nonmeaningful figures from memory when presented visually

Suggested Remedial Techniques for the ITPA

- A. Auditory Reception—understanding what is heard
    1. Listening games
    2. Give verbal directions and the child complies
    3. Tell a story or give a sentence and ask a question
    4. Ask questions that can be answered yes or no
    5. Use the Peabody Language Kit

6. Simon Says
7. Use Language Master
8. Tape recordings for sound training
9. Rhyming games
10. Conversation
11. Repetition games
12. Toy telephone—listen for identifying voices
13. Radio—weather, news, or commercials
14. Learn bird calls
15. Poetry with repetitive sections to be filled in by child
16. Records they can answer
17. Use alarm clock to signal important events
18. Rhythm band activities
19. Xylophone activities

B. Visual Reception—understanding what is seen
1. Identify objects in catalogues, magazines, or dictionaries
2. Identify colors, letters, geometric forms, etc.
3. Explaining action pictures
4. Tracing geometric forms
5. Outline figures
6. Use charts or maps
7. Sort objects with verbal assistance
8. Scrapbook of pictures which have been grouped
9. Cut out and paste pictures
10. Flashcards of colors, objects, people
11. Matching games, shapes, objects, colors
12. Copy designs
13. Match pictures to actual objects
14. Sightseeing trips
15. "Who is missing" game
16. Describe object or child—guess who
17. Place cards on desk or at lunch
18. Name cards for lockers or coat hooks
19. Pictures of various facial expressions
20. Follow directions—finger plays and action songs
21. Bingo with pictures or letters
22. Listen to a sentence and find its picture
23. Look at a word and find its picture

Diagnostic Tools and Prescriptive Planning

    24. Find missing parts
C. Auditory Vocal Association
    1. Scrapbooks or folders of pictures of opposites
    2. Collections of big and little pictures or objects
    3. Discrimination of sounds—high or low, near or far
    4. Use rhyming words
    5. Tell Me _____ what goes with various words (shoes, socks, etc.)
    6. Tell Me _____ many things that are blue, many things I can wear, etc.
    7. Riddles
    8. Folders of farm animals
    9. Weather posters
    10. Clothes for a winter day—bulletin board
    11. I am going on a trip—I will need (children make lists)
    12. Here is a leaf—tell me about it (and other objects)
    13. This is the Way We Wash Our Clothes (song)
    14. Old MacDonald Had a Farm (song)
    15. Name things that are made of cloth, wood, etc.
    16. Have children finish the story given orally
    17. What if—make up questions about hypothetical situations
    18. Language Lotto
    19. Peabody Language Kit
    20. Have children finish the sentence given orally
    21. Listen to a record; name the things that makes the sound
    22. Describe object; child must name and point to it
    23. Feel the object in the bag; describe it
D. Visual-Motor Association
    1. Sort and classify objects
    2. Show pictures—what comes next?
    3. Make a pattern—child reproduces it on peg board or paper
    4. Sort and classify pictures by categories
    5. Matching pictures to objects
    6. Matching numbers to pictures
    7. Matching words to pictures
    8. Connect the dots
    9. Reproducing shapes and figures

10. Color and identify objects
11. Which one is different in a series?
12. Sort clothing as to part of the body
13. Sort summer and winter clothing (actual or pictures)
14. Put toys or picture furniture in the right room
15. Card games matching furniture to room, rugs to rugs, chairs to chairs, etc.
16. Matching pictures of people to their work
17. Matching animals to their young and to their home
18. Goes together—pictures of things which go together are matched
19. Choose object which does not belong
20. Classification boxes—why do these go together?

E. Verbal Expressive (Vocal Encoding)
1. Show and tell
2. Picture dictionaries—tell about the picture
3. Pick an article to talk about
4. Pick a colored shape to discuss
5. Talk about picture books
6. Make a picture and tell about it
7. Follow directions—follow the leader orally
8. Guess what it is
9. Tell what you like best
10. Child gives directions to class—something to make, play, or do
11. Play school
12. Pretend to be someone or something—guess who?
13. Describe object in room—guess what it is
14. I am thinking of ―――――. What is it?
15. Show pictures and ask child questions about them
16. Have child finish story or sentence
17. Arrange pictures to tell a story
18. Give each child a picture and have him give some clues to help others identify it
19. I am going on a trip. I need to take ―――――. (Child must finish.)
20. What would you do if ―――――? (Use problem-solving situations.)

Diagnostic Tools and Prescriptive Planning

E. Manual Expressive (Motor Encoding)
   1. Imitate animal action
   2. Draw pictures on the blackboard
   3. Charades
   4. Simon Says
   5. Hokey Pokey
   6. Activity records and songs
   7. Have child demonstrate ideas
   8. Do as I do
   9. One child acts out animal actions and others guess
   10. Child chooses picture from grab bag and demonstrates what it can do
   11. Do as I say—from oral directions
   12. Pantomime any action; others guess what it is
   13. Fingerplays
   14. Build things with blocks
   15. Erector sets
   16. Role playing
   17. Lincoln Logs
   18. Act out familiar stories
   19. Puppets
   20. Songs—Here We Go Round the Mulberry Bush, Looby Loo, etc.
   21. Moving to music

F. Grammatical Closure
   1. Give simple directions
   2. Tape record instructions
   3. Language Master
   4. Activity songs
   5. "Do as I say" activities
   6. Finger plays
   7. Art activities
   8. Games using directions
   9. Activity to accompany records
   10. "May I"

G. Auditory Closure
   1. Fill in the missing word
   2. I am thinking of something—It is the fl--r.

3. Riddles
4. Hangman's Noose—Part of word is given. Child must fill it in. For each wrong guess part of a man is drawn, then the scaffold and noose.
5. I know a person named M--y.
6. I am an animal. I am a ch---en.
7. What is missing in a series?
8. Reproduce rhythms on drum
9. Finish the established pattern of drum beat
10. What is missing in a sentence?

H. Sound Blending
1. Rhyming
2. Complete familiar songs
3. Listen for sounds in records
4. Find something in this room that sounds like fl---
5. Find a b--e--d in the picture
6. Sound Lotto
7. Fill in the missing rhyming word
8. Fill in the missing word in a song
9. Choral reading
10. Finger plays

I. Visual Closure
1. Identify objects when shadow is shown
2. Identify children or objects from silhouette
3. Identify objects from rather clear ink blots
4. Find the hidden objects in pictures
5. Connect the dots
6. Complete the design by looking at the model
7. Guess what it is—part is missing
8. Puzzles in which each piece has a complete shape
9. Sewing cards
10. Finger painting
11. Make pictures from geometric shapes
12. Scribble pictures

J. Auditory Sequential Memory
1. Blindfold a child and ask him to tell from what direction a sound is coming, or what child in the class made a certain noise, or what animal the child is trying to imitate.

Diagnostic Tools and Prescriptive Planning

2. Give a series of words that rhyme with one word that does not rhyme. Examples: cat, rat, fat, foot; sit, hit, bin, bit.
3. Tap on desk, on glass, on paper, on blackboard, and on other objects in the room while children are looking the other way. They should try to name object tapped. A child could do the tapping with class guessing. The first to identify is the next to tap.
4. Blindfold one child and ask one of the others to call out his name. The blindfolded child tries to identify child who named him. Animal calls may be substituted.
5. Teach children jingles and nursery rhymes within their comprehension.
6. Give the children a direction for the purpose of executing some act. Later give two directions and then three, four, and five. The directions can be increased gradually and only as fast as the child can follow them successfully.
7. Tell the children a short story and have them repeat it as closely as possible to the original. Increase the length of the story.
8. Tap on desk with a pencil and ask children how many times you have tapped. Start out with two or three taps alternated irregularly, and increase the taps to four, five, and six.
9. Learn to play bells from numbers.
10. Name shapes, have children draw them.
11. Say numbers—first two, then more. Have child repeat or write them.
12. Name things on the grocery store shelf after hearing them.
13. I am going on a trip. I will take ——————.
14. I went on a trip and saw ——————. Each child adds one item.
15. What did you hear on the way to school?
16. Learn telephone numbers.
17. Record tapes of numbers for child to repeat or write.
18. Teach series of items to a puppet.
19. "Copy the Drum." Teacher taps a rhythm and child reproduces it.
20. Ten Little Indians.

21. Old MacDonald Had a Farm.
22. Fruit Basket Uspet.
23. Tell story and have child retell it.

K. Visual Sequential Memory
1. Copy bead series from memory.
2. Reproduce patterns from memory.
3. What comes next in the series of shapes?
4. Block designs.
5. Peg board patterns.
6. Stringing beads.
7. Show and Tell—What did you do after school?
8. Paper chains.
9. Make a calendar like the one on the board.
10. Many art projects—use different colored tiles or cubes to form pattern.
11. Parquetry designs.
12. Flash pattern—child reproduces it.
13. I went on a trip and saw a bird, a rabbit, and a cat. What did I see?
14. Touch It—I touch the desk, the chair, and the piano—You do it.
15. Duck, Duck, Goose.
16. Do as I do—Start with on activity, gradually add activities.
17. What is missing in the list?
18. What is missing in the doll house or picture?

A Word of Caution

This listing of sample diagnostic tools and some suggestions for planning remediation has not been intended as a complete recipe for all ills. Rather it has been given as a starting point from which to observe and devise plans for the child who is having learning problems.

The untrained observer may want to include the results of the Vineland Social Maturity Scale before attempting any program of improving the child's social behavior.

For further diagnostic tools the reader is referred to Oscar Buros' *Mental Measurements Yearbook*. Each diagnostic teacher will come to devise her own battery of instruments to fit her needs and the needs of the children with whom she will work. It is necessary to remember that the results of any of these instruments are indications and have not been handed down on a marble slab.

The creative teacher will use the suggestions given only as a beginning and will find many other techniques which are equally valuable.

Chapter VIII

PREVENTION OF LEARNING PROBLEMS

A REVIEW OF SOME of the modern approaches to teaching children with learning problems and a study of some of the older theories for teaching all children leads to the belief that there is little that is really new.

The classification and labelling of children is one innovation which is of questionable value. We begin as early as possible to screen classes and diagnose problems of children which may actually be problems of the parents, teacher, school, system, or society. Too often our diagnosis is for the purpose of placing the child in a special, labelled classroom where we presume he will receive special help with his problem. Often the diagnosis gives us a shield for our inability to teach the child and instead of alleviating his problem, we have succeeded only in marking him as a failure throughout his school years. Actually, we usually succeed in removing the problems from the regular classroom under the guise of providing special education and do only for the special child that which should be done for all children in their regular classrooms. Although the knowledge explosion implies that children have more to learn in less time, there has, as yet, been no technique discovered which will provide the child with more knowledge at birth. He must still learn as he grows.

Comenius, Locke, Rousseau, Seguin, and Itard were concerned with a better method for teaching children. They did not approve of rigid discipline or dull memorization and drill. They preferred to respect a child as a human being and assist him in learning. They believed that the senses were the path to learning and should be trained. The methods suggested by Comenius, Locke, and Rousseau were not designed for specific groups of children, rather for all children. Seguin and Itard addressed themselves to retarded children as did Montessori. Pestalozzi was concerned with waifs and children who would be labelled by modern educators as socially and culturally disadvantaged. The method of Montessori was used with the gifted as well as with the retarded.

By combining the educational principles of the early theorists who insisted upon training the senses as a prerequisite for further learning, we arrive at some current approaches to teaching. We are now concerned with education in early childhood. We hope to save time for the gifted and give the disadvantaged a head start. The Federal Government has provided funds to local programs for early childhood education, which was the plea of Pestalozzi. He hoped to improve society by improving the individuals in it.

There is evidence of interest in a multisensory approach to learning, but this is sporadic, insufficient, and often inefficient. This interest in sense training appears to be limited to children who have severe learning problems and is too often not applied until all else has failed. Educators who are concerned with children who have a learning disability use a multisensory approach, but not enough is done in the primary grades to educate the senses.

Teachers who work with children who have learning problems have learned to remove as many distractions as possible and, with Rousseau, prefer an environment removed from the mainstream of activity. This attitude is usually not reflected in the kindergarten and primary classes, where it should be of vital importance. The attitude seems rather to decorate all walls and add as many distractions as possible.

The idea of rewarding rather than punishing has been one educational principle inherited from earlier philosophers which appears to have widespread acceptance. Rewritten and relabelled it has become behavior modification. We seem to have forgotten that these thinkers were rebelling against extreme punishment but were not averse to humane punishment.

Comenius' idea that learning should begin with the concrete and then advance to the abstract was followed by Locke, Rousseau, Seguin, Itard, and Pestalozzi. This idea has been accepted by modern educators working with learning problems but seems to have been ignored or overlooked by many educators, particularly in the primary grades. Too often we proceed to the abstract, assuming that the concrete learnings have accidentally occurred.

Pestalozzi would recommend using the child's own experiences in his environment to help him learn. The application of this principle seems to be the exception rather than the rule. We seem to prefer to remove the maladjusted and the underprivileged from their environment as much as possible and place them in an artificial and unfamiliar one. We are expecting the child then to learn many new things at one time, not using his own environment and its experiences. Rather we should utilize the child's own familiar environment and thus make it possible for him to concentrate one one new learning at a time.

The early sense realists would have us attend to individual differences, teach each child only that for which he has been prepared, and allow him to proceed at his own rate. Today we modify this and call it individualized instruction or some similiar term and presume that it is a modern innovation.

The term motivation seems to have passed its peak of educational importance. Teachers often appear to be more concerned with salary, schedules, working conditions, fringe benefits, and manipulating people than they are with trying to help the child learn.

The teacher who works with children who have learning problems should resemble Pestalozzi's Gertrude. Pestalozzi would have insisted that any teacher, not just the special teacher, be a kind, warm, loving person. This teacher must have a sincere desire to learn from children in order to better assist them. All teachers have two eyes, but the good teacher uses hers differently. Details are noticed and understood. By observing and thinking about the observation, the teacher gains different approaches and techniques.

The newer methods of teaching which were reviewed appear to be extensions of the thinking of earlier sense realists. Maria Montessori paid particular attention to the materials to be used by the child in developing his senses. She considered sense training to be a prerequisite of higher intellectual functioning; and although her method was established for children of limited intelligence, it is currently being used for all children including the gifted. It would seem that Montessori has put into practice the educational principles of earlier thinkers.

The need for sense training was recognized by Alfred Strauss and Laura Lehtinen in their work with severely brain-injured children. Previously advocated techniques were used and new ones devised in an attempt to break sense training down into minute steps whereby the child could achieve success. Although the idea and the method were not an innovation, Strauss and Lehtinen were pioneers in that they were using the term brain-injured children. They were quite successful with this group of children, and the work is presently being carried on by Laura Lehtinen at Cove School in Evanston, Illinois.

After working and publishing a book with Strauss, Newell C. Kephart has continued his interest in sense training for children with a learning problem. At Purdue University he directed the Achievement Center for Children, where much work has been done with disabled learners. He developed a rating scale and training exercises to help teachers locate problem areas of motor activity and ameliorate them. His ideas provided the framework for the Winter Haven Program which was developed by a Purdue graduate student, Glen Lowder. Here again is the idea of perceptual training in early childhood before the mind becomes cluttered.

As seen in Chapter VII, there are many objective instruments which can be used to locate children who have not accidently developed their own senses and learned how to learn. In addition, there are many observable characteristics to be noted by a teacher or parent.

If we are concerned about the knowledge explosion and have a sincere desire to find some method whereby children who come into existence with so little can add so much in so short a time, it would behoove us to attend to the thinking of early sense realists and educational practices of Twentieth Century theorists. By identifying the learning problems and ameliorating them in early childhod, we could be helping the average child become more nearly gifted while helping the problem learner become average.

A PLAN FOR ACTION

To get a head start on learning and avoidance of problems it would seem wise to begin in a school of infancy as advocated by Rousseau. If individual problems are identified early, they are much easier to correct before they become learned incorrect patterns leading to undesirable solutions. Many of the problems children have do not obviously hamper their seeming success in primary learnings but do become a handicap to more advanced learnings.

Just having lived five or six years is the usual prerequisite for entering school, but this is unfair to all children. Every child deserves to start where he is, not where someone else thinks all children of five should be.

PRESCHOOL SCREENING should be done for every child who enters school, before he enters. Each school should have several diagnostic teachers who are equipped to do this testing. The children would be given the opportunity to demonstrate their abilities and disabilities on several different tools or instruments. These would need to be varied from time to time as some parents will buy the test and teach it to the child. Of the numerous instruments which have been designed for this purpose, only a few will be chosen as representative. Others may be found listed in Buros' *Mental Measurements Yearbook*.

Some screening instruments which could be used are the STAR, START, PPVT, PPRS, ITPA, Frostig Test of Visual Perception, Berry Buktenica Developmental Form Sequence, Wepman's Auditory Discrimination Test, and The Winter Haven Program. Although all of these will not be used with one child, each will be briefly described to encourage further investigation of the instrument.

STAR, or Screening Test of Academic Readiness, is published by Priority Innovations, Inc., P.O. Box 792, Skokie, Illinois 60076. This test was originally designed as a screening test for early entrance to kindergarten programs but has also been used in general kindergarten testing programs and in Head Start programs. STAR can be administered to fairly large groups of children in one test session. It is easily administered by teachers and is scored in six minutes. The results are not difficult to interpret, and children with unobservable learning problems can be screened out for further study.

START, or Screening Test for Assignment of Remedial Treatments, is a useful screening device specifically designed for preschool programs such as nursery school, Head Start, and kindergarten. Administered by teachers and scored in six minutes, it gives indications of strengths and weaknesses related to visual-auditory-motor-discrimination functioning. This test can be used with groups to find those children who are in need of special assistance in avoiding later learning problems. Development of visual memory, auditory memory, visual-motor coordination, and visual discrimination are assessed objectively. This is published by Priority Innovations, Inc.

PPVT, or Peabody Picture Vocabulary Test, is published by American Guidance Services. This is to be individually administered but not necessarily by a psychologist. It is designed to assess the intellectual maturity of persons between the ages of two and one-half and eighteen years. The child is asked to point to one picture among several when given a cue. The test is quickly administered and scored.

PPRS, or the Purdue Perceptual Rating Scale, by Roach and Kephart is published by Charles E. Merrill, Columbus, Ohio. This scale, which has been described in Chapter VII, should be used to screen those children whose breakdowns in the developmental sequence are not visible to the eye of the observer. This scale can be used individually or in a group situation and takes little practice in scoring.

ITPA, the Illinois Test of Psycholinguistic Abilities, has been described in Chapter VII, as has the *Frostig Test of Visual Perception* and *Wepman's Auditory Discrimination Test.*

The Beery Buktenica Developmental Form Sequence is published by Follett Publishing Company, 1010 Washington Blvd., Chicago, Illinois. The age range of this test is two to fifteen years, but it was designed primarily for the preschool and early primary grades. The purpose of this test is to assess the functional integration of visual perception and motor behavior in children, after determining specific areas of difference. The manual is to be used as a guide in providing corrective teaching techniques. The test consists of twenty-four geometric forms which are to be copied with pencil and paper. It can be administered individually or in a group situation by anyone who is able to read and follow the directions in the manual.

The *Winter Haven Program* includes a test to be used by the teacher for preschool screening. This can be obtained from the Lion's Club at Winter Haven, Florida. The children are shown seven geometric forms and are asked to finish them. Children who have visual motor problems may be identified by this test. The Lion's Club also publishes some suggested activities for amelioration.

AMELIORATION OF THE PROBLEMS

Children who have been found to have some problems which are deterrents to later learning should be given help as early as possible.

This should not be left to the judgment of the parents as is the usual situation. The parent must give approval before the child can receive special help. His lay opinion is often sufficient for determination of remediation.

Transition rooms or *junior kindergartens* should be established where equal opportunity is provided the child. Here he can be given the therapy needed to overcome his individual problem or problems.

In this junior kindergarten we must begin at the child's instructional level where he has much more success than failure. We should use a multisensory approach, developing increased refinement of all senses. Beginning with the concrete we should proceed slowly to the abstract and be careful to insure readiness for each new learning.

Experiences from the child's own environment should be utilized at every opportunity. Children could not be bussed from their natural environment to an unfamiliar one and still be expected to achieve success. Here we are changing the complete environment and expecting a child to adjust to the new one while living in entirely different surroundings. This only serves to confuse the child and compound his problems. It would seem wiser to use the child's own environment for learning experiences. In this way we might also be able to improve the environment instead of simply leading the child to believe that his natural environment is inferior and to be shunned. Exodus then becomes the only visible solution and this is unacceptable. Much more acceptable would be Pestalozzi's idea of improving society by assisting children to use experiences from their own surroundings and thereby improve the surroundings. Here, experiences are provided to ameliorate the experiential deficit.

This plan would require teachers who are specialists in the study of children as well as subject matter. This teacher is not one who feels that children with severe problems should be referred to a specialist for diagnostic work, hoping that he will need other services. This teacher is a specialist as well as a generalist. She must also be an integrationist and use all her specialized skills at every opportunity for the welfare of the individual child as well as the group. The group is smaller than the ordinary kindergarten to give her this opportunity.

Inefficient teaching is being eliminated as one of the causes of children's learning problems when we screen for unobservable difficulties and make provision for therapy. The multisensory approach for learning to learn and deliberate plans for ameliorating the deficit or weak areas must occur early in the life of the child if we intend to make an efficient learner from an inefficient one.

Although we would hope to overcome the problems of the child in the junior kindergarten, we must be realistic enough to realize that there would be a need for a transition room in most of the primary grades. Not all learning problems would be ameliorated in a junior kindergarten, so smaller classes should be provided at the various levels where intensified remediation can be provided. In this way we provide equal opportunity and not equal education for all children.

Appendix A

INSTRUCTIONAL MATERIAL SOURCES

ACLD RESOURCES
11291 McNab Street
Garden Grove, California 92641

H. W. ACTON COMPANY
New York, New York
  Number concept puzzles

ADDISON-WESLEY PUBLISHING COMPANY
School Division
3220 Porter Avenue
Palo Alto, California 94304
  Eicholz and O'Daffer, *Experiences with Geometry*, 1966.
  Basic Modern Mathematics, First Course, 1965.
  Basic Modern Mathematics, Second Course, 1965.
  Modern General Mathematics, 1964.

AERO PRODUCTS
St. Charles, Illinois
  Writing Fun Slates

ALLIED EDUCATION COUNCIL
P.O. Box 78
Galien, Michigan 49113
  The Fitzhugh Plus Program: Perceptual learning and understanding skills.

ALLYN AND BACON, INC.
470 Atlantic Avenue
Boston, Massachusetts 02210

AMERICAN ANNALS OF THE DEAF
Gallaudet College
Washington, D.C. 2000

AMERICAN BOOK COMPANY
Chicago, Illinois

Adventures in Dictionary Land, First through Fourth, by E. E. Lewis, Joseph Roemer, W. L. Matthew, Clifford Woody. For use with Webster's Dictionary.

AMERICAN EDUCATION PUBLICATIONS
Education Center
Columbus, Ohio
Know Your World. Newspaper for slow readers, Junior High School.

AMERICAN GUIDANCE SERVICES, INC.
720 Washington Avenue, S.E.
Minneapolis, Minnesota 55414

AMERICAN PRINTING HOUSE FOR THE BLIND
1839 Frankfort Avenue
Louisville, Kentucky 40200

PAUL S. AMIDON AND ASSOCIATES, INC.
5408 Chicago Avenue, South
Minneapolis, Minnesota 55417
Listen and Hear

ANN ARBOR PUBLISHERS
610 S. Forest Avenue
Ann Arbor, Michigan 48104
Visual Tracking by Robert Geake, Ph.D., Coordinator of Child Development Research, Greenfield Schools, and Donald E. P. Smith, Ph.D., Director of Reading Clinic, University of Michigan. A self-introduction workbook for perceptual skills in reading. This program is to develop visual discrimination and left to right direction.

ANTI-DEFAMATION LEAGUE OF B'NAI B'RITH
315 Lexington Avenue
New York, New York 10016

APPLETON-CENTURY-CROFTS
440 Park Avenue South
New York, New York

ARBOR PUBLISHING COMPANY
Campus Village
611 Church
Ann Arbor, Michigan 48104

ARCO PLAYING CARD COMPANY
Inexpensive games. May be purchased at dimestores, stationers,

drug stores, etc. Several different games, varying in style from Rummy to Old Maid, etc.

ART TONE PHOTO SERVICE, INC.
235 Rock Road
Glen Rock, New Jersey
  Flashlight Pointer

ARTS AND CRAFTS UNLIMITED
P.O. Box 572
Minneapolis, Minnesota 55440
  Tell and Draw Stories

ASSOCIATION FOR CHILDREN WITH LEARNING DISABILITIES
397 Moody Street
Wattham, Massachusetts 02154

ATTRIBUTES GAMES AND PROBLEMS
Elementary Science Study of Education
Development Center, Inc.
55 Chapel Street
Newton, Massachusetts 02160

BECKLEY-CARDY COMPANY
1900 North Narragansett Avenue
Chicago, Illinois 60639
  Rig-A-Jig

KEITH BEERY
2839 Heatherstone Drive
San Rafael, California 94903

BELL AND HOWELL CORPORATION
6800 McCormick Road
Chicago, Illinois 60645
  Language Master Machine

BENEFIC PRESS
1900 North Narragansett Avenue
Chicago, Illinois 60639
  Experimental Developmental Program

BOBS-MERRILL COMPANY
Test Division Company

Appendix A—Instructional Material Sources 119

4300 West 62nd Street
Indianapolis, Indiana 46206

CALIFORNIA ASSOCIATION FOR NEUROLOGICALLY HANDICAPPED CHILDREN
11291 McNab Street
Garden Grove, California 92640

CHILDCRAFT EQUIPMENT COMPANY, INC.
155 East 23rd Street
New York, New York

CHILDREN'S MUSIC CENTER, INC.
5373 West Pico Boulevard
Los Angeles, California 90019
Catalog on best records, books, rhythm instruments for exceptional children.

CHRONICLE GUIDANCE PUBLICATIONS, INC.
Moravia, New York

COLUMBIA UNIVERSITY
Bureau of Publications
Teachers College
525 West 120th Street
New York, New York 10000

CONCEPT RECORDS
North Bellmore
Long Island, New York 11100

CONSULTING PSYCHOLOGISTS PRESS
577 College Avenue
Palo Alto, California 94304
Frostig Test of Visual Perception and Administration and Scoring Manual: Developmental Test of Visual Perception, 1961. Teacher's Guide, 1964.

CONTINENTAL PRESS, INC.
Elizabethtown, Pennsylvania 17032

CONTROL DEVELOPMENT, INC.
1712 South Clifton Avenue
Park Ridge, Illinois 60068
Visual motor training—devices for eye-hand coordination using magnets.

CREATIVE PLAYTHINGS
P.O. Box 1100
Princeton, New Jersey 08540

CREATIVE PLAYTHINGS
Chicago, Illinois
  Arithmetic Tangibles

CREATIVE VISUALS
Division of Gamco Industries
Box 310
Big Springs, Texas

CUISENAIRE COMPANY OF AMERICA, INC.
235 East 50th Street
New York, New York

DAIGGER, A., AND COMPANY
Teaching Aids
159 West Kinzie Street
Chicago, Illinois 60610
  Learning Aids for Young Children (in accordance with Montessori methods)

DELAWARE VALLEY READING ASSOCIATION
610 Burton Road
Orland, Pennsylvania 19075
  Manual of Basic Reading Skills—A Guide for Teachers in Helping to Prevent Reading Problems, by A. W. Gomberg.

DEPARTMENT OF EXCEPTIONAL CHILDREN
School of Education
University of Southern California
Los Angeles, California 90007
  Engel, R., Reid, W., and Rucher, D., *Language Development Experiences for Young Children*, 1966.

DEPARTMENT OF SPECIAL EDUCATION
Superintendent of Public Instruction
316 South Second Street
Springfield, Illinois 62700

DEVELOPMENTAL LEARNING MATERIALS
3505 North Ashland Avenue
Chicago, Illinois 60657

Many materials for perceptual training and other materials devised for child with learning difficulties.

DEXTER AND WESTBROOK, LTD.
Rockville Center, New York
Instructional Aid Kits—reading comprehension, auditory comprehension.

DIMENSIONS PUBLISHING COMPANY
San Rafael, California 94903

EDUCATION PLAYTHINGS
American Crayon Company
Sandusky, Ohio

EDUCATION TEACHING AIDS
See A. Daigger listing.

EDUCATIONAL ACTIVITIES, INC.
Freeport, New York 11250

EDUCATIONAL DEVELOPMENT LABORATORIES, INC.
Division of McGraw-Hill Book Company
284 Pulaski Road
Huntington, New York 11744
EDL Controlled Reader. A reading program that includes a 35 mm filmstrip projector which presents material left to right or line by line fashion at an automatic rate. The program also includes workbooks to use in conjunction with the machine.

EDUCATIONAL PUBLISHING SERVICE
301 Vassar Street
Cambridge, Massachusetts
Orton, *A Guide to Teaching Phonics,* 1964.
Language Training for Adolescents—Gillingham Method.

EDUCATIONAL RECORD SALES
1621 North 31st Avenue
Melrose Park, Illinois
and
153 Chambers Street
New York, New York
"American Folk Songs for Children," "Do This, Do That," "Learn As We Play," "Sing Along," "Children's Songs," "Birds, Beasts, Bugs, and Little Fishes," and "Animal and Bird Songs for Children."

EDUCATIONAL SERVICE, INC.
P.O. Box 112
Benton Harbor, Michigan
Spark and *Plus*

EDUCATORS PROGRESS SERVICE
Randolph, Wisconsin 53956
Elementary Teachers Guide to Free Curriculum Materials, 1967.

EDUCATORS PUBLISHING SERVICE
301 Vassar Street
Cambridge, Massachusetts 02139
1. Singerland. *Screening Tests for Identifying Children with Specific Language Disability* (Grade 1 and beginning Grade 2; Grade 2 and beginning Grade 3; Grades 3 and 4), 1964.
2. Forbes. *Let's Start Phonics: Graded and Classified Spelling Tests for Teachers,* 1956.
3. Plunkett and Peck. *Spelling Workbook for Early Primary Corrective Work,* Book 1, Grade 2, 1960.
4. Childs and Childs. *Sound Spelling,* 1963;
Spelling Rules, 1965.
5. Plunkett. *Spelling Workbook for Corrective Drill,* 1961.
6. Helson. *A First Course in Phonic Reading,* 1965;
A Second Course in Phonic Reading, Books 1 and II, 1965.
7. Gillingham, A., and B. Stillman. *Remedial Training for Children with Specific Disability in Reading, Spelling, and Penmanship,* 1965.
Little Stories
Phonic Drill Cards
Phonic Word Cards
Dictionary Technique
Syllable Concept
Introduction to Diphthongs
Learning the Letters: A First Course in Phonic Reading
A Second Course in Phonic Reading
Sound Phonics
8. Bywaters, D. *Language Training for Adolescents: Curriculum Outline Student's Workbook*

ELEMENTARY SCIENCE STUDY OF EDUCATIONAL DEVELOPMENT CENTER, INC.
55 Chapel Street
Newton, Massachusetts 02160

Appendix A—Instructional Material Sources

FEARON PUBLISHERS
2165 Park Boulevard
Palo Alto, California 94306

FIELD EDUCATIONAL PUBLICATIONS, INC.
117 East Palatine Road
Palatin, Illinois 60067
Cyclo-Teacher Learning Aid, a device for programmed individualized instruction. High interest level—low reading level programs.

FOLLETT EDUCATIONAL CORPORATION
Chicago, Illinois
Frostig materials—Teacher's manual and workbooks

FOLLETT PUBLISHING COMPANY
1010 Washington Boulevard
Chicago, Illinois 60607

FROSTIG CENTER OF EDUCATIONAL THERAPY
7257 Melrose Avenue
Los Angeles, California 90046

GARRARD PUBLISHING COMPANY
Champaign, Illinois 61320
E. W. Dolch. *Sight Phrase Cards.* The cards are made from the ninety-five most common nouns and basic sight vocabulary.
E. W. Dolch. *The 10-Game.* A Dolch arithmetic game. This is a good game to practice addition combinations for 10.
E. W. Dolch. *Basic sight vocabulary cards.*

GOLDEN RECORDS
250 West 57th Street
New York, New York 10019
Stories in Sound, LP 202, Sound Effects by Sound-O-Rama.

GO MO PRODUCTS, INC.
Waterloo, Iowa 50704

JOHN D. HANKE
726 South College
Springfield, Illinois 62706
Instructional materials for handicapped children.

HARCOURT, BRACE AND WORLD, INC.
757 Third Avenue
New York, New York 10017

HARPER AND ROW
New York, New York

HARR WAGNER PUBLISHING COMPANY
609 Mission Street
San Francisco, California 94105
  The Time Machine Series
  The Jim Forest Readers
  American All
  Wildlife Adventure Series
  The Deep-sea Adventure Series
  Morgan Bay Mystery Series
  The Reading Motivated Series
  Checkered-flag Series

HAYES SCHOOL PUBLISHING COMPANY
321 Pennwood Avenue
Wilkinsburg, Pennsylvania 15221

HOLT, RINEHART, AND WINSTON, INC.
New York, New York
  Sounds and Patterns of Language—Talking Our Way to Reading, by Bill Martin, Jr., Truda T. Weil, Frances H. Kohen. Contains story-telling and discussion for first and second grade.

HOUGHTON MIFFLIN COMPANY
53 West 43rd Street
New York, New York 10036
  Listen and Do Phonics Program
  Learning Letter Sounds
  Learning Letter Sounds Filmstrips

HOUGHTON MIFFLIN COMPANY
Department M—110 Tremont Street
Boston, Massachusetts 02107
  The Letter Form Board

IDEAL SCHOOL SUPPLY COMPANY
11000 South Lavergne Avenue
Oak Lawn, Illinois 60453

ILLINOIS COLLEGE OF OPTOMETRY
3241 South Michigan Avenue
Chicago, Illinois 60601

Appendix A—Instructional Material Sources 125

**INSTRUCTIONAL MATERIALS AND
EQUIPMENT DISTRIBUTORS**
1415 Westwood Boulevard
California 90024
 Perceptual Communication Skills

INTERSTATE PRINTERS AND PUBLISHERS, INC.
Danville, Illinois 61832
 Text-Manual for Remedial Handwriting

INSTRUCTO CORPORATION
80 Cedar Hollow Road
Paoli, Pennsylvania 19301

THE INSTRUCTOR
Danville, New York 14437
 Arts and crafts for slow learners, games, stimulation games and activities for social studies, rhythmic activities.

**INTERNATIONAL FOUNDATION FOR EDUCATION
AND RESEARCH IN VISION**
Duncan, Oklahoma 73533

THE JUDY COMPANY
310 North Second Street
Minneapolis, Minnesota
 Stick-O-Mats
 Color-Shapes

KENWORTHY EDUCATIONAL SERVICE, INC.
Buffalo, New York
 The New Phonetic Word Drills, ten flip cards for learning twenty basic word families, initial sounds, and word endings.

KING COMPANY
4609 North Clark Street
Chicago, Illinois 60640
 The Bulletin Board, Primary Card File

THE MAKAR COMPANY
4 Palla Road
Carmel, New York 10512
 Primary Phonics
 Mac and Tab, Ted, The Wig

MARFEX ASSOCIATES, INC.
Box 510
Johnstown, Pennsylvania 15907
   Books and records useful for the slow learners or retarded readers. Materials for employment training with older childen. Catalogue of curiculum materials for the exceptional.

A. C. McBURG AND COMPANY
337 East Ontario Street
Chicago, Illinois 60611

McCORMICK-MATHERS PUBLISHING COMPANY, INC.
1440 E. English
Wichita, Kansas 67201

MEDIA
P.O. Box 2005
Van Nuys, California 91401

CHARLES E. MERRILL BOOKS, INC.
1300 Alum Creek Drive
Columbus, Ohio 43216
   Merrill Linguistic Readers

NOBLE AND NOBLE PUBLISHERS, INC.
750 Third Avenue
New York, New York 10037

PROGRAMS TO ACCELERATE SCHOOL SUCCESS, INC.
Box 1004
Minneapolis, Minnesota 55440
   The Physiology of Readiness by G. N. Getman.
   Visual Memory—Practice kit contains seventy-nine slides.

PARENTS' VOLUNTEER ASSOCIATION
1602 W. Broad Street
Columbus, Ohio
   Epps, R., G. McCammon, and Q. Simmons, *Teaching Devices for Children with Impaired Learning.*

PERCEPTION AIDS, INC.
930 Penobscot Building
Detroit, Michigan
   Educational aids for developing perceptual abilities necessary for learing to read and write.

Appendix A—Instructional Material Sources 127

PERCEPTUAL TRAINING ACTIVITIES HANDBOOK
TEACHER'S COLLEGE PRESS
Teacher's College, Columbia University
New York, New York
Betty Van Witsen

PHONOVISUAL PRODUCTS, INC.
P.O. Box 5625
Washington, D.C.
1. Phonovisual consonant workbook by Maud C. Stabbings, Ruth Larson Maverly, Wanda Stepalski Gaynes, and Ruth Bolen Montgomery.
2. Phonovisual vowel workbook.
There are other materials in the program dealing with phonics.

POTOMAC ENGINEERING CORPORATION
664 North Michigan Avenue
Chicago, Illinois 60611

THE PSYCHOLOGICAL CORPORATION
304 East 45th Street
New York, New York

PSYCHOLOGICAL TEST SPECIALISTS
Box 1441
Missoula, Montana
Graham-Kendall Memory for Design Test

RAND McNALLY
P.O. Box 7600
Chicago, Illinois 60680
General Offices:
8255 North Central Park Avenue
Skokie, Illinois 60076

RECORD CENTER
1616 North Pulaski Road
Chicago, Illinois 60639
Rhythms for Group Activities

PEEK PUBLICATION
4067 Transport Street
Palo Alto, California 94303
Audio-Visual Motor Training with Pattern Cards

RIL ELECTRONICS COMPANY
South Hampton, Pennsylvania 18966

ST. JOHN'S SCHOOL FOR THE DEAF
3680 S. Kinnickinnic
Milwaukee, Wisconsin 53207
    Sister Mary Walter, O.S.F., *Laugh and Learn with Julie and Jack, Building Stories with Julie and Jack, Writing Stories with Julie and Jack.*

SCHOLASTIC BOOK SERVICES
904 Sylvan Avenue
Englewood Cliffs, N.J.
    Studebaker and Studebaker, *Self-Teaching Arithmetic Books.*

SCIENCE RESEARCH ASSOCIATES, INC.
259 East Erie Street
Chicago, Illinois 60611
    Reading in High Gear
    New Rochester Occupational Reading Series
    Parker, D. H., *SRA Reading Laboratory, First through Seventh*

SCOTT, FORESMAN AND COMPANY
1900 East Lake Avenue
Glenview, Illinois 60025
    Arithmetic Cubes. Sixteen colored blocks with numerals, signs of operation and various placeholder symbols.

SILVER BURDETT COMPANY
Division of General Learning Corporation
Park Avenue and Columbia Road
Morristown, New Jersey 07960
    Pictures that Teach: Science for Beginners
    Pictures that Teach: Science I
    Primary Social Studies Picture Packets
    Families Around the World (Kindergarten)
    Families and Their Needs (Grade I)

SPECIAL CHILD PUBLICATIONS
Seattle Sequin Schools, Inc.
71 Columbia Street
Seattle, Washington 98104

Appendix A—Instructional Material Sources 129

SPEECH AND LANGUAGE MATERIALS, INC.
P.O. Box 721
Tulsa, Oklahoma 74101

STECK-VAUGHN COMPANY
P.O. Box 2028
Austin, Texas 78767
  Reading Essential Teaching Aids
  Sets of cards for developing phonic analyses of words
  Sets of primary grades

R. H. STONE PRODUCTS
Teaching Aids
Box 414
18279 Livernois
Detroit, Michigan 48221

TAPES UNLIMITED
13113 Puritan Avenue
Detroit, Michigan 48227
  Series of tapes to assist auditory perception skills.

TEACHERS COLLEGE PRESS
Columbia University
New York, New York 10027
  Russell, D., and E. Russell, Listening Aids Through the Grades, 1959.

TEACHERS PUBLISHING CORPORATION
Darien, Connecticut 06820
  Individualized Phonics—ditto masters.

TEACHING AIDS
Division of A. Daigger & Company
159 West Kinzie Street
Chicago, Illinois 60610
  Montessori Templates

TEACHING RESOURCES, INC.
334 Boylston Street
Boston, Massachusetts 02116
  Cheves, R., Visual Motor Perception Teaching Materials
  Erie Program #1, Perceptual-Motor Teaching Materials
  Fairbanks-Robinson Program #1, Perceptual-Motor Development

UNIVERSITY OF ILLINOIS PRESS
Urbana, Illinois 61801
McCarthy and Kirk, Illinois Test of Psycholinguistic Abilities

UNIVERSITY OF THE STATE OF NEW YORK
State Education Department
Bureau of Elementary Curriculum Development
Albany, New York 12224
Science for Children: K-3
Science for Children: 4-6
Social Studies: K-3

VISUAL PRODUCTS DIVISION
3M COMPANY
2501 Hudson Road
St. Paul, Minnesota 55119
Brown, J. F., Alphy's Show-and-Tell

VOLTA BUREAU
1537—35th Street, N.W.
Washington, D. C. 20000

GEORGE WAHR PUBLISHING COMPANY
Ann Arbor, Michigan
Hegge, Kirk, and Kirk, Remedial Reading Drills, 1965.

WEBSTER COMPANY
Manchester Road
Manchester, Missouri 63011
Tannenbaum and Stillman, Webster Beginner Science Series, 1960
Webster Classroom Science Library
It's Fun to Know Why
The Wonderful World of Science
Exploring Science

WEBSTER PUBLISHING COMPANY
1154 Reco Avenue
St. Louis, Missouri

WEBSTER DIVISION
McGraw-Hill Book Company
330 West 42nd Street
New York, New York 10036
Sullivan Associates, Programmed Reading

Sullivan Associates, Language Arts—Readiness Flip Chart Program from Behavior Research Laboratory dealing with direction, color, and letters of the alphabet.

WINTERHAVEN TEACHING MATERIALS
Winterhaven, Florida 33880

ZANER-BLOSER COMPANY
613 North Park Street
Columbus, Ohio 43215

THE LEARNING CENTER
Elementary School Department
Princeton, New Jersey 08540

LEARNING MATERIALS, INC.
100 East Ohio Street
Chicago, Illinois 60610

J. B. LIPPINCOTT COMPANY
East Washington Square
Philadelphia, Pennsylvania 19105

LYONS AND CARNAHAN
407 E. 25th Street
Chicago, Illinois 60616

THE MACMILLAN COMPANY
866 Third Avenue
New York, New York 10022
   The Bank Street Readers
   The Spectrum of Skills

MAFEX ASSOCIATES, INC.
Box 519
Johnstown, Pennsylvania 15907

MAICO COMPANY
Maico Building
Minneapolis, Minnesota 55400

MICHIGAN TRACKING PROGRAM
ANN ARBOR PUBLISHING COMPANY
610 South Forest
Ann Arbor, Michigan 48104
   Symbol Tracking, Letter Tracking, Word Tracking

MIDWEST VISUAL EQUIPMENT
571 West Randolph Street
Chicago, Illinois 60606

THE MILLS CENTER
1512 East Broward Boulevard
Ft. Lauderdale, Florida

MILTON BRADLEY COMPANY
Springfield, Massachusetts 01100

NATIONAL ASSOCIATION FOR CRIPPLED CHILDREN
2023 West Ogeden Avenue
Chicago, Illinois 60612

NEW YORK TIMES
100 Boylston Street
Boston, Massachusetts 02116
  Teaching resources, educational services.

NOBEL AND NOBEL PUBLISHERS, INC.
67 Irving Place
New York, New York 10003

Appendix B

SUGGESTED READINGS

Ashlock, P.: *Teaching Reading to Individuals with Learning Difficulties.* Springfield, Thomas, 1966.

Barsch, R.: *Achieving Perceptual-Motor Efficiency; A Space-Oriented Approach to Learning.* Seattle, Special Child Publications, 1967.

Bateman, Barbara: Learning disabilities, yesterday, today and tomorrow. *Exceptional Child,* December, 1964.

Beery, K. E.: Comprehensive research, evaluation, and assistance for exceptional children. *Exceptional Child, 35,* November, 1968.

Bender, Lauretta: *Psychopathology of Children with Organic Brain Disorders.* Springfield, Thomas, 1956.

Bond, G. L., and Tinker, M. A.: *Reading Difficulties: Their Diagnosis and Correction.* New York, Appleton-Century-Crofts, 1957 (Rev. 1967).

Brueckner, L. J., and Bond, G. L.: *The Diagnosis and Treatment of Learning Difficulties.* New York, Appleton-Century-Crofts, 1955.

Clemmens, Raymond L.: Minimal brain damage in children. *Children, 8:*179-183, September, 1961.

Crawford, John E.: *Children with Subtle Perceptual Motor Difficulties.* Pittsburg, Stanwix House, Inc., 1966.

Cruickshank, W.: *The Brain-Injured Child in the Home, School, and Community.* Syracuse, Syracuse University Press, 1967.

Cruickshank, W. (Ed.): *Psychology of Exceptional Children and Youth.* Englewood Cliffs, N. J., Prentice-Hall, 1963.

Cruickshank, W. (Ed.): *The Teacher of the Brain-Injured Child.* Syracuse, Syracuse University Press, 1966.

Cruickshank, W. M.; Bontzen, F. A.; Ratzegury, F. H., and Tannhauser, M. T.: *A Teaching Method for Brain-Injured and Hyperactive Children.* Syracuse, Syracuse University Press, 1961.

DeHirsch, Katrina; Jansky, Jeanette, and Langford, W.: *Predicting Reading Failure.* New York, Harper & Row, 1966.

Fernald, Grace M.: *Remedial Techniques in Basic Skill Subjects.* New York, McGraw-Hill, 1943.

Fouracre, Maurice H.: Learning characteristics of brain injured children. *Exceptional Child, 24,* January, 1958.

Frey, M. B.: A.B.C.'s for parents (of slow learners). *Rehab. Lit., 26,* No. 9, September, 1965.

Frierson, Edward C. (Ed.): *Educating Children with Learning Disabilities.* New York, Appleton-Century-Crofts, 1967.

Getman, G. N., and Kane, E. R.: *The Physiology of Readiness.* Minneapolis, Programs to Accelerate School Success, 1964.

Gillingham and Stillman: *Remedial Training for Children with Specific Disability in Reading, Spelling, and Penmanship.* Educator's Publishing Service, 1956.

Grzynkowicz, Wineva (Ed.): *Readings in Characteristics of Children with Learning Disabilities.* New York, Selected Academic Readings, 1968.

Grzynkowicz, Wineva, and Sturch, Jack E. (Eds.): *Diagnosis for Prescriptive Teaching.* New York, Selected Academic Readings, 1969.

Grzynkowicz, Wineva, and Sturch, Jack E. (Eds.): *Educational Therapy for Learning Disability.* New York, Selected Academic Readings, 1969.

Haring, N. G., and Phillips, E. L.: *Educating Emotionally Disturbed Children.* New York, McGraw-Hill Book Co., 1967.

Hewett, F.: *The Emotionally Disturbed Child in the Classroom.* Boston, Allyn and Bacon, 1968.

Hewett, F.: A hierarchy of educational tasks for children with learning disorders. *Exceptional Child,* December, 1964.

Kephart, N. C.: *Learning Disability: An Educational Adventure.* Lafayette, Ind., Kappa Delta Pi Press, 1968.

Kephart, N. C.: *The Slow Learner in the Classroom.* Columbus, Charles E. Merrill Books, Inc., 1960.

Lewis, P. A.: Implications of visual problems in learning disability. *Amer. Optometric Ass.,* February 26, 1961.

Marcus F.: *A Resources Book on Education of the Emotionally Handicapped Child.* Pleasant Hills, Calif., Contra Costa County Schools, 1963.

Monroe, G. E.: *Understanding Perceptual Differences.* Champaign, Stipes Publishing Co., 1967.

Otto, W., and McKenemy, R. A.: *Corrective and Remedial Teaching.* Boston, Houghton Mifflin Co., 1966.

Piaget, J.: *The Origins of Intelligence in Children.* New York, International University Press, 1952.

Radler, D. H., and Kephart, N. C.: *Success Through Play.* New York, Harper, 1960.

Appendix B—Suggested Reading

Rambush, Nancy M.: *Learning How to Learn.* New York, Taplinger, 1962.
Riesman, F.: *The Culturally Deprived Child.* New York, Harper, 1962.
Roswell, Florence, and Natchez, Gladys: *Reading Disability: Diagnosis and Treatment.* New York, Basic Books, 1964.
Russell, D. H., and Karp, Etta E.: *Reading Aids Through the Grades.* New York, Columbia University, Teachers College Press, 1959.
Semans, Sarah: Physical therapy for motor disorders resulting from brain damage. *Rehab. Lit., 20,* No. 4, 1959.
Spache, G. D.: *Good Reading for Poor Readers.* Scarsdale, N. Y., Garrard, 1966.
Stern, Catherine: *Children Discover Arithmetic: An Introduction to Structural Arithmetic.* New York, Harper, 1949.
Strauss, A. A., and Kephart, N. C.: *Psychopathology and Education of the Brain-Injured Child, Vol. II.* New York, Grune, 1965.
Strauss, A. A., and Lehtinen, Laura E.: *Psychopathology and Education of the Brain-Injured Child, Vol. I.* New York, Grune, 1947.
Sturch, Jack E., and Grzynkowicz, Wineva (Eds.): *The Socially Maladjusted and Culturally Disadvantaged, Vol. I and Vol. II.* New York, Selected Academic Readings, 1969.
Young, M.: *Teaching Children with Special Learning Needs.* New York, John Day, 1967.

INDEX

A
Acceptance, 59
Accommodation, 33
Adjustment, 4
Administrators, 64
Aggressiveness, 4
Assimilation, 33
Auditory acuity, 93
Auditory discrimination, 9, 26, 48
Auditory memory, 112
Auditory perception, 49

B
Balance, 92
Beery Buktenica Developmental Form Sequence, 113
Behavior, 4, 11, 38, 40, 59, 63, 73
Betts, Emmet A., 53
Bullying, 5

C
Classroom, task oriented, 60
Cognitive development, 32
Comenius, 15-17, 42, 54, 108, 109
Compassion, 58
Conceptual difficulties, 13
Creativity, 59
Culturally disadvantaged, 1, 6, 7
Culture, 6
Curriculum, 3, 39, 59

D
Daily program
 intermediate, 71
 older children, 71
 primary, 70
Dedication, 63
Delinquent, 2
Developmental lag, 3, 6, 8, 13, 65
Developmental sequence, 36
Diagnosis, 68, 108
Diagnostic teacher, 90
Diagnostic tools, 106
Digestive disturbances, 4
Diplomacy, 60
Discipline, 19, 27, 72, 73, 108

Discriminations, 22
Dishonesty, 5
Disinhibition, 11
Distractibility, 11
Disturbances in sleep patterns, 5

E
Educational principles, 25
Emotional disturbance, 4
Emotional instability, 12
Environment, 4-9, 14, 18-22, 25-35, 41-46, 50, 54, 58, 110, 114
Experiential deficit, 3, 6, 8, 14, 65, 114
Eye-hand coordination, 25, 92
Eye-motor coordination, 26
Eye movements, 92

F
Flexibility, 59
Form perception, 92
Frostig, Marianne, 69
Frostig Test of Visual Perception, 113

G
Gesell, Arnold, 36-40, 52
Getman, Dr. G. N., 91
Goals, 5, 6, 14, 58, 72
Grammar, 16

H
Home visits, 67
Hyperactivity, 12
Hypoactivity, 12

I
ITPA, 98, 113
Individual differences, 36
Instructional level, 54, 114
Integration, 74
Intellectual development, 33, 39
Intelligence, 33, 34
Intuitive thought, 34, 35
Itard, Jean, 15, 23, 109

J
Junior kindergarten, 115

Index

K
Kane, Dr. Elmer R., 91
Kephart, Newell C., 50-54, 96, 111
Keystone Telebinocular, 90

L
Language, 44
Learning disability, 1, 10, 11, 13, 14, 16, 24, 26
Lehtinen, Laura, 46, 47, 49, 50, 110, 111
Lincoln-Oseretsky, 97
Locke, John, 15-19, 54, 108, 109
Lowder, Dr. Glenn, 52, 53, 54, 111

M
Maladjusted, 110
Maladjustment, 4, 6, 36
Marianne Frostig Developmental Test of Visual Perception, 93
McQuarrie, Dr. Charles, 53
Memory, 20
Mentally deficient, 15
Minimal brain dysfunction, 10
Montessori, 41-45, 51, 108-110
Motivation, 20, 30, 58, 110
Motor behavior, 113
Motor coordination, 40
Motor disturbances, 12
Motor education, 43, 44
Motor efficiency, 94
Motor pattern, 51
Motor training, 24
Movement, 19, 24, 37
Multidisciplinary approach, 24
Multisensory approach, 26, 40, 109, 114
Music, 25

N
Neurologically impaired, 13

O
Objectives, 69
Operational stage, 35

P
PPVT, 113
Parents, 67, 68
Perception, 18, 20, 21, 22, 26, 56
Perceptual discrimination, 51
Perceptual disorders, 12
Perceptual distortion, 26
Perceptual motor training, 54
Perceptual training, 53, 111
Permissiveness, 58, 60
Perseveration, 11
Pestalozzi, 15, 21, 22, 54, 108, 109, 110
Phonics, 9, 47
Physiological training, 25
Piaget, 32-40
Preconceptual thought, 34
Preoperational stage, 34
Preparation, 61
Preschool screening, 112
Psychiatrist, 2
Psychoeducational Inventory of Basic Learning Abilities, 94
Public relations, 75
Punishment, 18, 31, 109
Purdue Perceptual Motor Survey, 51, 96, 113

R
Rapport, 30, 57
Readiness, 16, 18, 20, 22, 29, 47, 48, 114
Realism, 58
Reason, 21
Reasoning, 20, 35
Reflection, 17
Remedial techniques
 ITPA, 99, 100, 101, 102, 103, 104, 105, 106
 WISC, 79, 80, 81, 82, 83, 84, 85, 86, 87, 88, 89, 90
Remediation, 68, 76, 77, 106, 114, 115
Respect, 59, 69
Restlessness, 4
Rewards, 17, 28
Roach, Eugene G., 96
Rousseau, 15, 19, 54, 108, 109, 111

S
Seguin, 15, 24, 108, 109
Sensation, 17, 18, 19, 22, 26
Sense impression, 21, 22

Sense organs, 25
Sense training, 15, 16, 19, 20, 21, 23, 24, 41, 44, 110, 111
Sensitivity, 5
Sensorimotor activities, 53
Sensorimotor processes, 51
Sensorimotor stage, 34
Sensorimotor system, 50
Sensorimotor training, 40, 54, 55
Sensory deprivation, 3, 6, 8, 65
Sensory education, 25, 43
Sensory perceptions, 21
Sloane, William, 97
Socially maladjusted, 1, 3, 5
Spatial relationships, 28, 54
Speech, 4
Speech and language disorders, 12
STAR, 112
START, 112
Stealing, 4
Strauss, Alfred, 46, 47, 49, 50, 110, 111

T
Tactile education, 44
Teacher, 56-69, 74, 114
Teacher training, 61

Teaching aid, 18
Tics, 4
Transition rooms, 114

U
Underachiever, 1, 2, 3

V
Valett, Robert, 94
Vineland Social Maturity Scale, 106
Visual acuity, 90
Visual aids, 17
Visual discrimination, 113
Visual image, 28
Visual memory, 93, 112
Visual motor coordination, 113
Visual motor problems, 113
Visual perception, 21, 47, 54, 91, 113
Visual-perceptual distortion, 27

W
WISC, 77
WPPSI, 79
Wepman Auditory Discrimination Test, 93, 113
Winter Haven Program, 52, 53, 111, 113
Writing, 16, 18, 22, 25, 44, 45, 48